No More Tears

God's Punch Line

The Key is Love

Let Go and Let God

Christ is the Center

Live By Faith!

Living in Wonder & Praise

Christ is Our Hope

Say the Word!

Bless the Lord, O My Soul

The Lord is My Rock

On Eagles' Wings

At The King's Table

Daily Walk With Jesus

Crash Course in Mormonism

2

NO MORE TEARS

Volker Heide

King of Kings Publishing
Madison, Connecticut

4

Foreword

This book can give you a true hope in Jesus Christ. The good news of God's kingdom declares you can have the forgiveness of sins and a new life in Jesus. He is the Savior who deeply loves you. In this troubled world, the Son of God is our only true hope.

These sermons look at many favorite Bible readings and you should read the passages listed beforehand. Spend some time reading these passages. Note the context to get a better understanding of the text.

The Word of God is powerful and effective. God cares about you and promises to provide for all of your needs. Let these sermons lead you deeper into the Word of God.

Read the Bible every day and carefully study the Scriptures. The Holy Spirit will show you the answers you are looking for. In Christ, there is always hope!

6

NO MORE TEARS

Featuring:

FILLED WITH THE HOLY SPIRIT: ACTS 2:1-21 9

I SAY TO YOU, ARISE! MARK 5:21-43 17

THE TRANSFORMER: JOHN 2:1-11 28

CHECK THE ROCK! MATTHEW 28:1-10 34

LOST AND FOUND: LUKE 15:1-24 41

THE MAIN THING: 1 THESSALONIANS: 1:1-10 48

INCREASE OUR FAITH! LUKE 17:1-10 55

NO MORE TEARS: JOHN 11:17-44 61

THE END OF YOUR ROPE: 1 KINGS 19:1-21 69

LIKE A ROARING LION: 1 PETER 5:6-11 76

THE LORD IS MY SHEPHERD: PSALM 23:1-6 82

A CAREER CHANGE: MATTHEW 3:13-17 87

SUPERNATURAL! JOHN 20:19-31 94

A LESSON IN GIVING: MARK 12:38-44 102

THE SON SETS YOU FREE: JOHN 8:31-36 108

A GLIMPSE OF HEAVEN: REVELATION 7:9-17 115

RAISING CAIN: GENESIS 4:1-15 122

BE STRONG IN THE LORD: EPHESIANS 6:10-20 129

DON'T MISS THE POINT: MARK 11:1-10 134

DEPEND ON GOD: LUKE 12:22-34 140

DO NOT BE AFRAID: MATTHEW 10:24-33 146

A TRICKY THING: LUKE 17:11-19 154

AN UP AND DOWN LIFE: JOHN 16:5-33 161

8

IN THE CROSS OF CHRIST I GLORY: JOHN 3:1-21	168
AT THE KING'S TABLE: LUKE 22:7-38	174
BELIEVING THE SCRIPTURES: JOHN 2:13-22	182
SOMETHING TO CELEBRATE: ZEPHANIAH 3:14-20	190
WHAT HAPPENED THAT FRIDAY: LUKE 23:26-49	197
THEOLOGICAL TERMS	207

FILLED WITH THE HOLY SPIRIT: ACTS 2:1-21

A father took his son for his first worship service at a local church. When it was over the father asked his son, "Well, how did you like the service?" The boy replied, "It was great! I can hardly wait to go again." The father was surprised, so he asked, "What did you like best? Was it the sermon?" The boy shook his head and said, "No." "Was it the people?" "No." "Was it the music and hymns?" "No." "Well then, what was it?" asked the father. The boy smiled and said, "When they passed around those plates, I got twenty dollars. What did you get?"

Clearly, here is a case of miscommunication. There is a lot of that going on today. Even though we live in a world of smartphones, emails, Twitter, Facebook and Instagram, there is still so much misunderstanding and confusion. It's very hard to communicate with others in a way that is clear, concise and comprehensible.

Do you remember the story of the tower of Babel in Genesis 11? When God created humanity, there was only one language, a common speech that all of humanity shared.

Back then, we could communicate effectively because everyone spoke the same language.

I am sure you have had that experience of trying to learn a foreign language. Most of us have tried to learn a language in junior high or even earlier. We had our Spanish or French classes. You know how frustrating that can be, trying to learn to communicate effectively through a foreign language. Our original parents did not have this problem. Adam and Eve, and all of their descendants after them, had one common language. (I am guessing that was Hebrew.)

Yet, the tower of Babel reveals how we used our communication abilities to once again rebel against our Creator. We joined together to worship ourselves. We turned away from the God who made us, and united our efforts to try to elevate ourselves above our Maker.

Therefore, the Lord God intervened into that situation and the common speech of humanity was disrupted. God mixed up the language of all the people there, and because people could not communicate effectively anymore, they were scattered all over the earth. From now on, humanity would be divided into different cultures, societies, languages, and dialects. Such a division would lead to a lack of communication. It would also lead to disunity, conflict, prejudice, hatred and discord – all those things that are so familiar to us today.

But now, something extraordinary occurs. We are told that on the Day of Pentecost, there were staying in Jerusalem, people from every nation under heaven. You had folks from all over the world that had come to Jerusalem to celebrate the great festival of Pentecost (also known as the Feast of Weeks). This was a harvest festival that occurred seven weeks after the Passover. It was a time of celebration of God's creation and his rich blessings. It was a time of joy and thanksgiving. The first-fruits of the harvest would be dedicated to the Lord, the Maker of heaven and earth.

Luke says, "When the day of Pentecost arrived, the disciples were all together in one place. And suddenly there came from heaven a sound like a mighty rushing wind, and it filled the entire house where they were sitting. And divided tongues as of fire appeared to them and rested on each one of them. And they were all filled with the Holy Spirit, and began to speak in tongues as the Spirit gave them utterance."

The Day of Pentecost is marked by God's gift. There came directly from heaven the mighty gift of the promised Holy Spirit. The Spirit comes with wind and fire. That wind is the very breath of life that makes us living beings. The flames of fire are the real presence of God, just like the pillar of fire that led the people of Israel out of Egypt and through the wilderness.

And the Holy Spirit bestows upon the disciples the gift of tongues.

Tongues are that ability to suddenly speak a new foreign language. And all of these people visiting Jerusalem hear the disciples speaking in their own language. They said, "We hear them talking in our own tongues and declaring the mighty works of God." And all of these people were perplexed and amazed. They said, "What does this all mean?"

That is when Peter stood up and addressed the crowd. Peter quotes from the prophet Joel to show that God is doing a new thing here. God is overcoming the confusion that occurred at the tower of Babel. Peter says that the Holy Spirit of God will be poured out on all people – upon our sons and daughters, upon young and old, male and female – all people of this entire world. And we shall now speak of the mighty wonders of God. We will tell of the great works of our Creator. We will share the good news of the gospel with everyone.

The Holy Spirit will overcome all the barriers and boundaries that separate people today. The Spirit of God will overcome all the things that divide us, and together we will declare the great wonders of God. That is the Holy Spirit's work, that is his job. He enables us to hear the gospel and believe the message about Jesus. Then, we are able to share the gift we have received. We can communicate God's message to others. We share the gospel with all people – everyone.

That is what Pentecost is all about. The Holy Spirit overcomes the differences that separate us, and he creates a unity in the faith we share. Just look at our congregation. We all come from many different backgrounds. We were all born in different places and at different times. Some of us grew up in loving and caring families. Others had a childhood filled with hurt and pain. Some have a happy marriage; others have experienced broken relationships. Some have had successful careers; others have experienced frustration and disappointment. Some have been healthy all their life; some have experienced multiple health problems and sickness. Some of us are happy and content; others are having a hard time and struggle each day.

Yet, by the grace of God, we are all here together to hear the Word of God. We have gathered to worship our Savior and to give thanks for his many blessings. And as we worship and hear the Word of God, the Holy Spirit is poured out upon us. We personally experience the mighty works of God. We are filled with the Holy Spirit. Grace is bestowed and sins are forgiven.

God does his mighty work in us, and the Holy Spirit leads us to the cross of Jesus. There, on Mount Calvary, we clearly see the love of

God revealed as the Son of God gives himself for us. We see how our Lord wins for us that gift of forgiveness. Jesus gave himself for us as he died on the cross.

Then, the Holy Spirit leads us to the empty tomb, and we discover that Christ has risen from the dead. Our Lord has conquered death for us. He has broken the power of evil and has defeated the devil. Through his resurrection, we now have the victory. The risen Lord is the first-fruits of the resurrection, and he bestows this gift of a new life upon all who believe in him.

The Holy Spirit now takes us to the ascension of our Lord, and we watch how Jesus returns to the Father, he ascends into the skies. He goes to prepare a place for us in heaven. The Holy Spirit opens our eyes to see all the wonders of God's grace, and he opens our hearts to receive God's love. That love of God, so powerfully revealed through the cross and resurrection of his Son, now flows into our hearts like streams of living water. We now discover that "everyone who calls on the name of the Lord will be saved."

By faith, we are filled with the Holy Spirit, and the Spirit unites us in the faith we share. We are the communion of saints. The Spirit brings us together in the universal church, which covers the entire world. We are joined together with Christians all around the globe, in Africa and Australia, in America and the Far East, in South America and the Pacific islands – in every nation on this earth. The Spirit has been able to overcome all the barriers and boundaries of a divided humanity.

The Holy Spirit creates the one language of faith, the language of the cross, resurrection and ascension of Jesus Christ, the Son of God. Now, we all speak the same tongue, this new speech of faith in Jesus. The communication is clear. You now comprehend this message: God loves you! God forgives you. He erases and removes all the mistakes and failures of your life that bother you so much. That is gone. For the sake of Christ, you are forgiven!

And the Father now gives you a new life – a life that will never end, a life where the fire of God's presence burns brightly in your heart. A mighty rushing wind sweeps away your fears, and you once again discover that you have the courage and strength you need to deal with all the problems you are facing right now. The risen Lord bestows his power and grace upon you. These are the mighty works of God, which we experience by faith.

We have experienced the wonders of God. We have heard the Word. The message has been received. God's communication to us today is clear and direct. We listen, hear and comprehend what the Lord is telling us. We believe the gospel and call upon the name of the Lord. We are saved and born again.

Today is our Pentecost. Let us now join together and with one voice give thanks to our God and Savior. Let us rejoice in our Creator and celebrate that we are filled with the Holy Spirit. And let us tell others of the good news of a Savior who loved us and who gave himself for us. We now declare with one tongue, the mighty works of God, the Maker of heaven and earth. We tell others that there is hope - there is a powerful hope for a world divided by hatred and discord - there is the promised Holy Spirit, the gift the Father bestows upon lost sinners like you and me.

By the power and grace of the Holy Spirit, we become different people, people who now follow the way of Christ. This is the way of love and forgiveness, the way of grace and mercy, the way of service and sacrifice, the way of humility and peace. We now share this good news with all people.

We want to share God's message with the entire world. We seek for everyone to hear, comprehend and believe the gospel message of God's love in Christ. We tell others about God's gift. We speak and declare to all people that Christ has risen. We communicate that powerful promise that "everyone who calls on the name of the Lord will be saved." Amen!

I SAY TO YOU, ARISE! MARK 5:21-43

Today, we see Jesus in action. We see how our Lord bestows his gift of healing and help. He reaches out to various people who are hurting and broken. Jesus takes us by the hand, and he says, "I say to you, arise!"

In our reading for today, we see the family of a 12-year-old girl. A desperate father seeks help for his dying child. His family is in great distress. Imagine how they felt. We also see a woman struggling with an on-going health problem. She has been to endless doctors, but was no better for it. She had undergone numerous medical treatments, but she actually grew worse. It seemed as if no one could help her. With whom do you identify the most in today's reading? It is easy to see ourselves in this story. We can understand what these people were going through because we have felt their pain.

First, there is the great crowd that gathers around Jesus, all eager to be near him. These people all come to the Lord seeking healing and hope. They are clamoring to be near Christ because they know he has the power to help them. They are hurting. Then there are the twelve disciples who seem confused and overwhelmed by all these events. They fail to understand what Jesus is all about. There is also the woman in the crowd who silently bears the burden of her sickness. And there is Jairus and his wife. Their child will end up dying. The people will gather at his house, weeping and crying over this great tragedy. The sting of death will touch this family.

We can all identify with these people in our reading. We have all struggled with the burdens of life. We have been confused and overwhelmed by problems. We have cried out for help. We have dealt with sickness and pain. We have experienced the death of our loved ones.

We have felt the desperation of Jairus who cried out to Jesus, "My little daughter is at the point of death! Come and lay your hands on her, so that she may be made well and live." We have also felt the silent struggle of the woman who was sick for so many years. She had to deal with her painful condition every day of her life. She could not find relief from her suffering. She woke up every morning and nothing had changed for her.

All of these people come to Jesus. Today, we do the same. We reach out to the Son of God, and we cry out, "Lord Jesus, help me! Lay your healing and helping hands upon me! O Lord, remember me in your mercy and grace, so that I may be made well and be saved." Today, we reach out by faith and we touch the garment of

Christ. We discover the power of God at work for our salvation. We hear his word, "Talitha cumi, I say to you, arise!" We again realize that our Lord has the power to bestow healing and life. There is hope!

We see that so clearly towards the end of our reading, when Jesus reaches the house of Jairus. A great crowd of people are weeping and wailing. They act as if all is lost and there is no hope. Jesus says, "Why are you making such a commotion and weeping so much? The child is not dead, but is sleeping." However, the people laughed at Jesus when he calls death "sleep."

However, think about this: Through the power of Christ, death is no more permanent than falling asleep. Death is like falling asleep, and then waking up to a bright new morning in heaven. Through Christ, we pass through death to a new life in heaven, a life bright with the sunshine of God's love. The sting of death is not permanent. It does not have the last word. Jesus does.

We now see how Christ goes into the room where the dead girl was lying on a bed. He takes her by the hand and says, "Talitha cumi! Little girl, I say to you, arise!" Immediately, the girl sat up, got out of bed, and began to walk around the room. Jesus then told her parents to give her something to eat. She was alive – give her some food. Our Lord speaks his Word and his life-giving power is so clearly revealed. The Son of God speaks the same Word to us. At our baptism, Jesus said, "Talitha cumi! I say to you, arise!" And the power of the Holy Spirit was bestowed. You were given the new birth through the water and the Word. You were born again by the power of the Triune God. You were "quickened" and made spiritually alive.

This spiritual life is now nourished and fed every time we gather to worship. Every week, the risen Lord says, "I will give you something to eat." He feeds us with his Word and with his Supper. He gives us the Bread of Life. Christ bestows grace through Word and Sacrament. He feeds our soul with his wondrous gifts.

At worship, our Lord says, "Talitha cumi! I say to you, arise. Receive my body and blood, given and shed for you. Hear the Word, which I proclaim. Receive the gift I bestow upon you." Here, in this sanctuary, the risen Christ feeds us with the Bread of Life. He feeds our hungry heart. He nourishes our soul with the Word of God and Holy Communion.

Here is the heartbeat of our spiritual life. At worship each week, we confess our sins and receive absolution. We confess our brokenness and failures. The Lord then proclaims, "I say to you, arise! Your sins are forgiven." Every week, we come to hear this gospel message. We are raised up into the new life, which the Son of God bestows upon us by his wondrous grace.

This weekly cycle continues for us throughout our life. We feed upon the Bread of Life, and are quickened by the Holy Spirit's power. Finally, there will come that day when we reach the end of this earthly life. We will pass through the gates of death. We will depart to be with the Lord forevermore.

And when the last day comes, when the final judgment takes place, the Lord Jesus will once again say to each of us, "Talitha cumi! I say to you, arise! Enter the resurrection life I have won for you." Then, our bodies will be raised from the dead by the incredible power of God. We will be glorified and transformed. We will fully enter the true life, which God intends for his children to have forever.

This will be a new life filled with unending joy and happiness. There will be no suffering and sickness. There will be no more sadness or grief. No more pain and heartache. No more death - no more tears! Let's be honest: Death is the most terrible thing we will ever have to face. Death is our worst enemy.

The sting of death brings the deepest pain and loss we will ever experience. We know that death was not a part of God's original creation. Death did not exist until Adam and Eve sinned. Their sin broke the perfect relationship we had with our Creator. Their rebellion ruined a perfect creation. They brought death into existence through their fall.

And so, ever since the fall, we have had to deal with the brokenness of life. We have had to struggle with on-going sickness and the death of our loved ones. We have had suffering and misery, pain and woe, grief and heartache, endless tears and sadness. Look again now and see how Jesus comes onto the scene. Great crowds gather around him because they knew that something special was happening here.

That is why Jairus came to him. This is why the woman in the crowd reached out to touch the garment of Christ as he passed by. All of these people heard reports of how Jesus healed the sick. They all knew that Christ had the power of God to help us. They had faith. They trusted that the Lord could do something about their problem.

Jairus pleads for Jesus to come as quickly as possible. He is in dire need. He says, "My little daughter is dying. Come quickly and heal her!" And Jesus says, "Okay, let's go!" However, as they were pressing through the great crowd, something unusual happens. The woman who had been sick for so many years pushes through the press of people, so that she can at least reach out and touch Jesus as he passes by. She wants to touch his garment because she has faith in the Messiah of Israel.

This suffering woman demonstrates a strong faith that would not give up. She knew that Jesus had the power to help her. She believed that he could do something about her terrible condition. She said, "If I can just touch Jesus as he goes by me, I know I will be helped."

The Lord immediately felt his power go out from him, and so he stops - he stops dead in his tracks. "Who touched my garment?" Jesus calls out to the crowd. Finally, the woman comes forth, and she tells what had happened to her. She tells the Lord what she did. Notice how Jesus leads her to confess her faith publicly. "For it is with your heart that you believe and are justified, and it is with your mouth that you confess and are saved."

The Lord Jesus now smiles, and he says, "Daughter, your faith has made you well! Go in peace and be healed of your disease." We can just picture this powerful scene of how Christ calls this woman forth, and how she finally confesses her faith. Jesus then says, "Go in peace! Your faith has made you well."

However, just as Jesus was saying this, some bad news arrives. Several people come from the home of Jairus, and they tell him, "Your daughter is dead. Why bother the teacher any further?" However, when the Lord hears this, he immediately tells Jairus, "Do not fear! Only believe." That is what we need to hear today. Jesus says to each of us, "Do not be afraid! I know what you are facing in your life right now. Don't be afraid! Just believe. Have faith! Trust that I can help you."

Our Lord points to himself, and he shows us how he has the power to conquer sickness and death. Our Lord has the power to undo the curse that Adam and Eve brought into this creation. He is able to heal our sickness and take away our death. But this happens only through his cross and resurrection. Such healing occurs only because Christ takes our sickness upon himself. Life comes to us only because the Son of God has experienced our death. God himself suffers that sting. God himself takes upon himself the curse of sin and death. That is what happened when Jesus died on the cross.

Our Lord is the Son of God. And even though he is true God in every way, he humbles himself. He lays aside his divine glory and honor, and he becomes our servant. Paul says, "You know the grace of our Lord Jesus Christ that though he was rich, yet for your sake he became poor, so that you by his poverty might become rich."

That is the message of the cross: Christ humbled himself and gave up the riches of his divine glory. He becomes poor as he enters the poverty of our death. He died for us so that we might be made rich with the grace of God. The Son of God suffered and died for you. Through his sacrifice, your sins are forgiven! Through his atoning death, your guilt is taken away. Through his resurrection, the light of God's love shines upon you. A new morning dawns and everything changes for us. The sting of death is taken away. The victory is yours today. Listen: Christ has risen! He has risen indeed. Alleluia!

"Talitha cumi! I say to you, arise!" Arise and enter the new life Jesus Christ has won for you. Lay aside all of your doubts and fears. Put away your confusion and unbelief. Reach out now and touch his garment. Believe in Christ and joyfully confess your faith. There is a blessed healing to be found in the blood of Jesus, a spiritual healing of mind and soul. This is the powerful gift of knowing that you are always safe in God's love. "By his wounds, you are healed." "Go in peace! Your faith has made you well."

Our heavenly Father overwhelms us with his mercy and grace. The steadfast love of the Lord never ceases. His mercies never end. His compassion fills our hearts, and his love fills our souls. We now sing for joy because Christ has come into our life. We sing, "Great is thy faithfulness!"

A family was on a summer vacation. They were travelling across the county in their car. One morning, as they were driving with the windows open, a big wasp got into the car. The wasp was buzzing around inside. The little girl in the backseat was terrified. She had always been afraid of bees and wasps, and so she cries out, "Daddy, help me! The wasp is going to sting me!"

The father quickly pulls the car over to the side of the road. He waits until the wasp comes toward him and is buzzing against the front windshield. That is when the father reached out and caught the wasp in his cupped hands. He held the wasp until he felt a sting. Then, he let the wasp go. The little girl saw the wasp flying around the car again, and she cried out, "Daddy, the wasp is going to get me!" But the father said, "No honey, it can't hurt you anymore. Look at my hand!" And he showed her the stinger from the wasp. It was in his hand. The girl was safe. The danger was over.

And so it is for us. The sting of death has been removed. The power of sin is broken. We are now safe and secure because our Lord has taken that sting upon himself. We are safe. Death cannot hurt us anymore. We have the victory through the cross and resurrection of the Son of God. He became poor so that we might become rich.

Paul says, "Where, O death, is your victory? Where, O death, is your sting? The sting of death is sin, and the power of sin is the law. But thanks be to God! He gives us the victory through our Lord Jesus Christ."

Like the father in our story, Jesus says, "Look at my hands!" Jesus says, "See the mark of the nails. See how I took the sting of death for you. It can't hurt you anymore. You are safe in my love! I now bestow upon you eternal life."

This is why we rejoice and sing today. This is why we give thanks and praise our gracious heavenly Father. Together sing, "Great is thy faithfulness! Morning by morning, new mercies I see. All I have needed, thy hand hath provided. Great is thy faithfulness, Lord unto me."

The Lord Jesus Christ has come to bestow healing and hope. He reaches out to those who are hurting and broken. He comes to those who are desperate. He truly has the power to help you in your time of need. He loves you with a steadfast love that never ceases. He gives you a new life that will never end.

Jesus says, "Talitha cumi! I say to you, arise! Your faith has made you well. Go in peace and serve your heavenly Father. Do not fear, but keep on believing. Do not be afraid, but trust that I am with you forevermore." Amen!

THE TRANSFORMER: John 2:1-11

Today we look at John's story of a big wedding celebration at Cana in Galilee. Jesus and his disciples go to the wedding reception and something goes wrong. Weddings are great opportunities for celebration, but they seldom go off without a hitch. You've seen those video clips of the many things that can go wrong at a wedding. The best man faints. The bride stumbles and falls. Someone forgets the rings. The pastor's robe catches fire. A cell phone goes off in the middle of the vows. These things may cause us to laugh, but we move on because we know the important part of a wedding, the love of the couple and their commitment to the wedding vows.

Weddings were a big deal during the time of Jesus. The ceremony would take place late in the evening. The father of the bride would take his daughter on his arm, and with the wedding party in tow, they would parade through the streets of the town, taking the longest route, so that everyone could come out, see the wedding party and congratulate the bride.

Finally, the wedding party would arrive at the home of the groom. The wedding actually took place in front of the groom's house. Then, they had the festivities that sometimes lasted for days. It was a time of great celebration for the entire town. Jesus and his disciples were invited to just such a celebration. However, just as they arrive, disaster strikes. After the party begins, word comes that they have run out of wine. This was a terrible situation, causing great embarrassment to both families involved. They would be totally upset. We can almost hear them saying, "Our wedding is totally ruined! We are supposed to be filled with joy and happiness, but now, this happens."

For whatever reason, Mary, the mother of Jesus, got involved in this wine problem. We don't know why. Maybe it was the wedding of a friend or relative. However, Mary knew what to do. She knew where to go. We can almost hear Mary saying, "Don't worry about it, I'll talk to my son. He can fix anything."

Therefore, when Jesus arrives at the wedding party, Mary comes up to him and says, "They have run out of wine." He responds, "Wait a minute, what does this have to do with me? My hour has not yet come." Now, why does Jesus say that? "My hour has not yet come." What does that mean?

Mary doesn't blink an eye. She simply turns to the servants standing there, and says, "Do whatever he tells you." Jesus tells the servants, "Fill the jars with water." And they filled them up to the brim. Each of these big jars held about 30 gallons of water, and there were six jars. (That is about 180 gallons of water.)

Jesus then told them to draw some out and take it to the master of the banquet. They drew it out of the jars and when it was tasted, everyone discovered that the water was transformed into the finest wine you have ever tasted. You suddenly have 180 gallons of the best wine ever tasted.

Why so much wine? Here we see how our Lord is an extravagant giver. He never gives just a little; he always gives superabundantly, an overflowing blessing. We see the same thing when Jesus fed the hungry crowds. He multiplied five loaves and two fish so that 5,000 people and their families ate. And when everyone had eaten their fill, they had twelve baskets of bread and fish left over. Jesus gave them more than they could possibly eat. It was superabundant.

This great abundance of bread, fish and wine shows us how God's grace just overflows into our life. It fills our hearts and souls to the brim. However, this miracle also shows us something else very interesting. First, and most obviously, the ordinary water was transformed into the best of wine. The power of Christ is clearly revealed. But secondly, the disciples were transformed. They were changed.

Remember, our Lord has just begun his ministry. He has just called these disciples to follow him. And John tells us that through this miracle, Christ manifested his glory to them. Jesus showed them that he truly is the Son of God. The disciples saw this miracle and they believed. This action revealed the power of the Messiah. The glory of the Lord was revealed to them, and they were transformed by this.

So, what does all this mean for us? It means that if Jesus can change water into wine, he can change us, too. He can change our doubt into saving faith. He can change our depression into hope, our anger into love, and our sorrow into joy. He can turn our sin into forgiveness and our death into eternal life. His power can do all things. This miracle shows us that. Change is possible because Christ has the power to work miracles.

Our Lord Jesus is the Transformer. Through his abundant grace, we are transformed from plain old water into the finest of all wines. Christ changes us, and he changes us from the inside out. But how exactly does this happen? How does this occur?

Notice again how Jesus told his mother at first, "My hour has not yet come." He says that several times in John's Gospel as he works his way to the cross. "My hour has not yet come."

But right after the Palm Sunday entrance, just before the passion begins, Jesus declared to all the people, "Now the hour has come for the Son of Man to be glorified. Now the hour has come! When I am lifted up from the earth, I will draw all men to myself." The hour finally came for Jesus to be glorified. He would be glorified as he is lifted up on the cross, as he dies for the sins of the world. However, this glory was hidden at first. It was hidden under the pain and suffering of Jesus, hidden under darkness and defeat, hidden under his death and burial.

The disciples could not see the glory of God on Good Friday. At the time of the crucifixion, all they could see was gloom and despair. Only the Easter resurrection would later reveal what really happened. And the exact same thing occurred when Jesus turned the water into wine. At first, it looked like nothing special had occurred. Only after the wine was drawn out of the jars and tasted, only then, was it discovered that a miracle had happened. You had to taste; then you could see. Taste and see!

The same thing happens on Good Friday. At first, it looked like only a terrible, senseless death had occurred. All you see is death and loss. However, when Jesus is drawn out of the tomb, we discover that a miracle has occurred. We taste and see that the Lord is good. Christ has risen! And he is the best wine we have ever tasted!

Christ manifests his glory to us through his cross and resurrection. He shows how he has transformed our death into eternal life. He defeats the power of death and the devil. His resurrection has changed our sorrow into joy. He has opened our eyes to see his true glory. This is the Son of God who was lifted up on that cross. He has drawn us to himself. And as the Lord draws us to himself, he transforms us. We are changed forever. We are now disciples who joyfully confess that Jesus is the true Son of God. We taste and see that the Lord is good.

Today, the risen Lord invites us to his wedding celebration. He invites us to his grand party where we receive his gifts and celebrate with great joy and gladness. At this wedding feast, Christ feeds us with his true body and blood. We taste and see, and discover once again the miracle of Holy Communion. The Lord superabundantly blesses us with his gifts. Christ empowers us to go forth and share his blessing with others.

Today, we taste of the Lord's grace and favor. We see the glory of God. And we rejoice that in Christ, we always have hope. Come now and partake of his banquet. Come and receive his gifts! Amen!

CHECK THE ROCK! Matthew 28:1-10

Matthew is the only Gospel that mentions how the tomb of Jesus was sealed with a guard. On Saturday, the chief priests go to Pilate and request that a guard be posted at the tomb, so that nobody would tamper with it. The Romans post the guard, seal the rock and guard it through the night.

Our message today is: "We need to check the rock, watch it roll away and become a part of the resurrection of Jesus Christ." Then, the incredible power of his resurrection will change you forever. You will experience the new and abundant life that God freely gives. The first thing you need to do today is "Check the rock."

In a big national park in California, there is a rope, which has a big rock hanging from it. A large sign sits next to it to explain this unusual device. The sign says, "This rock on a rope is our Weather Station. Check the rock! If the rock is wet, it's raining. If the rock is swinging, it's windy. If the rock is dry, it's sunshine. If you can't see the rock, it's foggy. If the rock has been blown away, it's a tornado. If the rock is jiggling about, it is an earthquake. Check the rock!"

This sign shares a powerful truth: "Check the rock!" Many of us have come to church today with questions on our minds. We have come searching for answers and looking for truth. We are looking for something to change our life for the better. Life can sometimes be so confusing. We wonder why things are so hard for us. What makes life worth living? Why am I here? What's it all about anyway? That statement, "Check the rock," can help us find some answers.

+ Are you wondering what your life is all about? Check the rock!

+ Are you wondering how to be set free from fear? Check the rock!

+ Are you wondering if God's Word is true? Check the rock!

+ Are you wondering how you can make a new beginning? Check the rock!

+ Are you wondering what makes life really worth living? Check the rock!

When the women went to the tomb early on Easter morning, the position of the rock was the first clue that something spectacular had happened. The big rock was moved out of the way, to open things up. When they checked the rock, they discovered it had been moved. Furthermore, we need to not only check the rock, but we need to see for ourselves that the tomb is empty. The story of Jesus doesn't provide us with much hope if the tomb is not empty. In fact, if Christ were still lying dead in his tomb, we would be left with absolutely nothing. We would still be lost and dead in our sins. If Christ never rose from the dead, we would have no hope at all.

Picture the scene on Good Friday. Death is all around. Jesus has been killed. The cries of his followers can be heard throughout Jerusalem. Their grief is very real and deep. Christ had died, and he was buried and the tomb is tightly sealed. It all looks so hopeless.

We all know that feeling. We all know what it is like to lose someone close to us. Our grief can be overwhelming. The death of someone we love can devastate us like nothing else in this world. Matthew says that the woman went out early on Sunday morning to take a look at the tomb. In other words, they were doing something we have done many times ourselves, travelling to the cemetery to visit the gravesite of a loved one.

We all know what it is like when a loved one dies and is buried. All that is left is a grave or a tomb, a headstone or a marker. It seems like there is no hope when you standing all alone in the cemetery. But wait! You have to check the rock, watch it roll away, and then discover that the tomb of Jesus is empty. That totally changes everything! That's what Easter does.

It changes us. It changes the deep sadness of death into the powerful joy of the resurrection. When you check the rock, you discover it has been moved by the incredible power of God. An earthquake shook the ground and an angel of the Lord descended from heaven to roll back the stone and sit on it. (That is a nice touch, the angel sitting on top of the stone. That is a striking detail in this amazing story.)

The real point of the angel's appearance was the message he delivered to the women, "Do not be afraid, for I know that you seek Jesus who was crucified. He is not here! He has risen, just as he said. See the place where he lay."

"He has risen, just as he said." Christ is alive! He has defeated death. He has kept his promise to rise again, and he wants you to now walk into the tomb, and see for yourself. That is why the angel rolls back the stone, so that everyone could see the tomb is empty. He is not here because he is alive. This resurrection of Christ validates his gospel message: It's all true! It's for real. It's genuine.

And this gospel can change your life forever. Now the resurrection from the dead becomes possible for you. Everlasting salvation becomes your reality. And your loved ones are not lost, but you will see them again in the glory of heaven. These promises of God are unlocked for all who come to the open tomb.

Now that the rock has been rolled away, we can look inside and behold the power of our Lord. His resurrection tells us all things are now possible. It shows us that God's Word is always true, even when we think otherwise.

I once saw a poster called, "OUR THINKING VERSUS GOD'S WORD." This poster shows us that our thinking is not always correct when it comes to what the Almighty Lord can do. We underestimate our God. We fail to realize the incredible power of his Word.

+ We think: "It's impossible." God says: "All things are possible."

+ We think: "I'm too tired." God says: "I will give you rest."

+ We think: "Nobody loves me." God says: "I love you."

+ We think: "I can't go on." God says: "My grace is sufficient for you."

+ We think: "I can't figure things out." God says: "I will direct your steps."

+ We think: "I can't do it." God says: "You can do all things through me."

+ We think: "I can't manage." God says: "I will supply all your needs."

+ We think: "I worry too much." God says: "Cast all your cares on me."

+ We think: "I'm not smart enough." God says: "I will give you wisdom."

+ We think: "I'm all alone." God says: "I will never leave you or forsake you."

These are God's promises to you. How can you tell if all of this is true? Check the rock, watch it roll away, and behold the resurrection of Jesus! Far too many people today are afraid to trust anyone or anything anymore. They are fearful of what tomorrow may bring. They are so wrapped up in loneliness, worry and grief, their life has no meaning or joy. However, here is the key to having a meaningful life: Jesus Christ. He is your Lord and Savior.

Life is worth living because Jesus is alive. He is the Lord of your life, and he deeply loves you. You have been raised up with Christ. You now belong to him. And he will never leave you or forsake you. He will abide with you, forever.

Christ will give you strength and power. He will give you rest for your soul. He will give you wisdom, direction and purpose in life. He will give you grace. Make the resurrection of Christ your own today. Check the rock and see how it has been rolled away. Look and see, the tomb is open and it is empty! God's Word is true.

Rejoice and give thanks! Christ has risen and he has risen for you. Go now in peace and live in his power each day. Trust in the risen Lord and he will bless you every day. Christ has risen! Thanks be to God! Amen!

LOST AND FOUND: Luke 15:1-24

We begin today with a story. Two hunters went up to Alaska to do some big game hunting. The game warden warned them that they might get lost. He told them, "If you get lost, fire three shots in rapid succession. I will then come and find you."

Well, sure enough, they did get lost. The first hunter said to the other one, "You'd better fire those three shots." Therefore, he did. But nothing happened. They waited a while, and then the first hunter said, "You'd better fire three more shots." And so he did. Again, nothing happened. This was repeated, several times. Three shots, nothing happened. Finally, the first hunter said, "Look, it's getting dark and we're really lost. You'd better fire three more shots." And the second hunter said, "I can't. I've run out of arrows!"

I hate it when I get lost. Especially when I drive down to Long Island to visit my daughters, I will get lost. The towns and expressways all look the same after a while. You get turned around and confused. You lose your bearings. Or else I will lose something I need. I can't find my car keys when I have to leave the house. I cannot find my wallet. Where are my glasses? Where's that note I wrote to myself so that I wouldn't forget that important thing I have to do today?

Today, Jesus tells some stories about being lost. All of these stories talk about the same thing: Something is completely lost, and then, it is suddenly found. This discovery results in great joy and celebration. Jesus says, "Suppose you had 100 sheep and one of them gets lost. Would you leave the other 99 sheep unattended, just to go searching for that one lost sheep? Would you make an all-out effort to find that one lost sheep, when you already have 99 all safe and sound?"

Christ then asks, "If you had ten silver dollars in your house, and you lose one of them, what would you do? Would you turn your house upside down looking for that coin? Would you take all of your furniture out onto the front lawn, tear up all the carpet and turn your whole house completely upside down, just to find that one single coin? And when you suddenly discover that lost coin, would you call up all your friends and neighbors, and throw a great big party just to celebrate?"

Then Jesus tells the story of about a young man who is rude and rebellious. He rejects his father and family. He demands his share of his inheritance and leaves home. He goes far away, and they lose all contact with him.

Perhaps it was just as well because the young man got into all kinds of trouble.

Gambling, alcohol and drugs: a parent's worst nightmare. Finally, the son hits rock bottom. When he finally comes home, he does so in shame and disgrace. But what does the father do? The father runs down the street to welcome and hug his lost son. He then throws the biggest party that anyone has ever seen to celebrate.

All these stories of Jesus are over the top. No one would ever consider it worthwhile to turn the whole house upside down to look for one lost coin. No one would leave 99 sheep behind, just to search for one that foolishly got lost. No one would throw a party for an irresponsible kid who ruined his life. No one would ever do such a thing. No one, that is, except God. Our God is full of surprises. He does the most unexpected and surprising things. God does what we would never do.

The truth is we live in a throwaway world. If something breaks, we throw it away. If the toaster breaks, we throw it away and buy another one. If we lose our sunglasses, we don't waste a lot of time looking for them; we just go and buy another pair. If we lose some change from our pocket, we don't worry about it. Pocket change isn't worth much anyway.

However, these stories Jesus tells are in direct contrast to the throwaway world we live in. Our God is different. If someone is in trouble, God is concerned. If someone gets lost, he is searching for them. If we are broken and damaged, God doesn't just throw us away.

God has an obsession about each and every person living in this world. And God doesn't want a single person to be lost. Everyone is special. That is why God will go to any length to seek out and save the lost. In fact, you can say that God specializes in finding what is lost, fixing what is broken, repairing what is damaged, and rescuing those who are perishing. That is the gospel message of all these stories Jesus tells. You are deeply loved by gracious God! Moreover, everyone has value in God's eyes, a value that cannot be measured.

Furthermore, God's love will go to any length to save us. His love never gives up. God keeps on loving us, no matter what we have done. Like the father in the story of the prodigal son, God is waiting for you to return to him.

Do you remember how that story went? The father loved his son so very much. He never gave up on his child. His love never faltered, even as he waited day after day, looking down the road, watching for just a glimpse of his son coming back home. And the father didn't put any conditions on his son's return. He didn't say, "If you clean up your act, then you can come home." No, he loved him, and he loved him unconditionally. He was prepared to take that chance of forgiving him. He was prepared to welcome back his wayward son, even though the son hadn't done anything to deserve it.

Look again at the beginning of our text. Do you see what it says? "Tax collectors and sinners were all drawing near to hear Jesus teach. But the Pharisees and scribes complained about this. They grumbled and said, 'Look at this! This man receives sinners and eats with them.'"

Imagine that! The Pharisees and scribes are actually upset and angry because Jesus was sharing the Gospel with the lost. "This man welcomes sinners and eats with them." Jesus was reaching to those who were considered the very dregs of society – outcasts like tax collectors, prostitutes, bums and losers - people who had totally lost their moral compass. But notice that Jesus was also reaching out to the Pharisees and scribes as well.

In fact, all of these stories were told directly to the Pharisees and scribes to get them to realize that God cares about all people. And these stories about the lost coin, the lost sheep, and the lost son remind us that we are lost, too. We are no different from those tax collectors, prostitutes, bums and losers that Jesus encountered. We are sinners as well.

In addition, we also need to hear the Gospel. We also need to discover the message of God's love for the lost. We also need to experience the powerful, amazing love of our gracious God. That is why the Son of God came into this world - to show us that God loves all people, and God wants all to be saved. God's love reaches out to the lost, and it grabs hold of all people, especially those who are broken or hurting inside.

Our Lord wants us to realize that even though we are sinners, God still loves us. Even though we've made a mess of our lives, God doesn't give up on us. Even though we do not deserve it, God still loves us, and he graciously forgives all of our sins. Such forgiveness is possible because the Son of God was willing to go to the cross for us. There, upon that cross, Jesus became lost. He became lost, so that we might be found. He was forsaken, so that we might be accepted. He entered the depths of hell, so that we might experience heaven. He died on that cross, so that we might live.

Our Lord has paid the price for our sins. He carried our heavy burden and suffered our brokenness. Through his atoning sacrifice, we are healed and restored; we now receive a new and better life. "By his wounds, you are healed."

No wonder there is a lot of celebrating going on in Luke 15. Whenever something that was lost is found, there's a party. The shepherd who finds the lost sheep comes home, saying, "I am so happy I found my lost sheep. Let us celebrate!" The woman who finds her lost coin throws a big party, too. When the prodigal son returns home, the father says, "This son of mine was dead, but now he is alive. He was lost, but now is found. Come on, let's celebrate and be glad!"

Today, we acknowledge our sinfulness. We confess we have repeatedly made a mess of our life. We are broken, bruised and banged up. We are hurting inside. And the truth is we continually get lost and lose our bearings. But listen, "Jesus receives sinners and eats with them." This means Jesus welcomes and receives us! He reaches out to us today with the good news of the Gospel. He searches, seeks out and saves those who are lost.

Now, the Savior invites us to his Holy Supper. The Lord Jesus graciously welcomes sinners back into God's family. We were dead, but now we are alive. We were lost, but now, we are found. Therefore, open your heart to receive God's gift. Rejoice that we are invited to his Table where he feeds us with his true body and blood. The Son of God receives us back into his company. Grace is bestowed and sinners are forgiven. The grand party is now underway. Come on, let us celebrate! Amen!

THE MAIN THING: 1 Thessalonians: 1:1-10

Three women die and all three reach heaven at the same time. There, they meet St. Peter. He tells them he has some important business to take care of and asks them to wait outside. Finally, after a long while, he returns and calls the first woman into his office.

He apologizes for making her wait so long. "Oh, I don't mind at all," she says, "I'm just thrilled to be here." Peter is delighted by her attitude. He says, "Well then, if you can just answer one more question for me, we can finish processing your papers. Now tell me, how do you spell, 'God'?" The woman spells it for him, and she enters the gates of heaven.

St. Peter calls in the next woman and also apologizes for making her wait. "Oh, I don't mind," she says, "It's certainly worth the wait." Peter is pleased. He says, "Okay, if you can answer one more question, we can finish up here. Tell me, how do you spell, 'God'?" The woman spells it, and she enters heaven.

Finally, Peter calls in the third woman. He also apologizes to her, but she refuses to accept his apology. "That was quite rude," she says, "you making me wait like that. All my life I have had to wait. I wait in the checkout line, I wait in traffic, I wait at the doctor's office, I wait for the kids to get home from school, and now you expect me to wait to get into heaven? Well, I just won't stand for it!" Peter says, "I'm so sorry you had to wait like that. If you can just answer one more question, we can finish up here. Tell me, how do you spell, 'Kyrgyzstan'?"

There are a lot of silly jokes about heaven. They usually feature Peter, pearly gates, people waiting in lines, and other stereotypes. I hope you realize that this is not what the Bible teaches. Heaven is a reality that is beyond our ability to imagine or describe. It is far more wonderful and awesome than we could ever expect or comprehend.

St. Augustine, the great teacher of the early church, was once discussing heaven with several of his students. They all had the usual questions people have: "What will it be like? What kind of bodies will we have? Will we recognize other people? What about eating and sleeping?" On and on the questions went. Finally, Augustine said, "Look, you are missing the main thing. All those questions are fine, but the main thing is, 'How do I get there?'"

How do we get to heaven? That's the main thing. How do we enter eternal life? How can we be saved? What must we do? And can anybody really be certain of their salvation? This reminds me of something you've probably heard before. It goes like this. Suppose you were to die tonight. You suddenly find yourself standing before the judgment seat of God. God then asks you, "Why should I let you in heaven?" What would you say? Think about it. If God were to say to you, "Why should I let you enter heaven?" what would you say?

Most people would probably say, "Well, I deserve to go to heaven because I'm not so bad. I am a good person. I have never done anything that bad. I try to do what's right." However, the truth is we are not such good people. When we stand before the judgment seat of God, our true condition is revealed. We are not good. In fact, we are just the opposite.

We are sinners and we have a real problem with anger, lust, greed, jealousy, pride, hatred, and selfishness. We struggle to do what's right. In fact, we find it much easier to do what's wrong. The truth is we constantly rebel against God and question his wisdom and ways.

The truth is that we don't deserve to go to heaven. Instead, we deserve to go to hell. We deserve to be punished for our sins. Deep down inside, we know that is true. We know that we are not good or wonderful people. We are all lost and fallen sinners.

If we try to pretend this is not the case, we are only putting lipstick on a pig. If we think we can go to heaven because we are good and deserve it, we are kidding ourselves. The truth is not in us. What we need to do is simply stand before God and confess, "Lord, have mercy on me, a sinner!"

In addition, if God were to ask you, "Why should I let you into heaven?" you should simply answer, "Because you gave your Son to suffer and die for me." You see, that is the main thing: Jesus. He is the One who rescues lost sinners. He is the One who suffers our punishment. He suffers our hell and damnation, so that we might enter God's new creation and have eternal life.

"For God so loved the world that he gave his only Son, so that whoever believes in him should not perish, but have eternal life." That is the main thing: Jesus. He is the One we point to when we stand before the judgment seat of God. Our Lord gives us that certainty of knowing that we are loved by God, and our sins are totally and absolutely forgiven. This undeserved love of God now puts our hearts at rest. It lifts us up on eagles' wings. It bestows peace and serenity. We now have that reassurance that we are always safe in God's love.

Today, we hear the Apostle Paul speak of this in 1 Thessalonians. He says, "My dear friends, we know you are loved by God and that he has chosen you." Notice how Paul says,

"You are loved by God. He has chosen you." Now, think about that! God loves you, and he has chosen you by grace to be his child. Isn't that amazing?

Paul then continues, "We know this is so because our Gospel came to you not just in words, but also in power and in the Holy Spirit and with full conviction." Paul speaks of the power of God's Word and the power of the Holy Spirit who brings full conviction. The Bible is not just information. It is not just facts like you might see in a magazine or read in a newspaper. The Word of God is the very power of God, his power unto salvation.

The Word delivers Christ straight into our hearts. The Holy Spirit works through this Word of God to create saving faith within us. The Spirit leads us to the cross and empty tomb. The Spirit brings us to faith. That is the Holy Spirit's job. And when this happens, God fills our hearts with certainty and conviction. We now know that salvation is a free gift. And God's gifts always bestow joy and confidence, even in the face of suffering and hardship.

Remember that Paul was writing to the people who were experiencing great hardship and difficulty. These new Christians were being persecuted for their faith. They were struggling to get by and were having a tough time. Yet, even in the midst of all this suffering, Paul could say to them, "You received the

Word of God, even as you were experiencing much affliction. But you received that Word with the joy of the Holy Spirit."

Paul says the Holy Spirit worked through God's Word to create faith, love and hope in the lives of the Thessalonians. The Holy Spirit gave them endurance and the ability to put their faith to work. And the same thing happens for us. The Spirit of God kindles a saving faith in our hearts, and this faith is a busy and active thing.

Paul says, "We always thank God for all of you, mentioning you in our prayers. We continually remember before our God and Father, your work prompted by faith, your labor prompted by love, and your endurance inspired by hope in our Lord Jesus Christ."

"You have become an example to all the believers in Macedonia and Achaia. They hear how you turned away from false idols, and have turned to God. You now serve the Living God as you wait for his Son from heaven. The Father raised his Son from the dead. This is Jesus who delivers us from the coming wrath."

Here again, Paul leads us back to Christ, back to the Savior who delivers us from our sins and the depths of hell. That is why Jesus Christ is our hope, our certainty and confidence. Like the Thessalonians, we receive the Gospel and turn to God. We joyfully put our faith in the Lord Jesus, and that makes all the difference.

Even in the face of suffering and tough times, we turn to the Lord for help and deliverance. He is the true Son of God and he is our Savior.

Now, we stop putting our faith in ourselves. We can stop thinking that we deserve to go to heaven, or that somehow we have to merit God's love. We let go of all those false notions, and we just relax and accept God's free gift.

That is when we discover the true joy of the Holy Spirit. We discover the amazing power of God's Word. We experience the certainty and conviction of eternal salvation. Now, we learn to live by faith, and we simply trust that God is in control of all things, even our salvation. Now, our faith becomes active in works of love and mercy. Our labor is prompted by God's love. Our endurance is inspired by the hope of eternal salvation we have in Christ.

That is the main thing: Salvation is a free gift given by God's grace in Jesus Christ, the Son of God. I go to heaven only because of Jesus. He is the only Savior, and I know that he loves me and forgives me. He is the main thing and the only thing that matters in the end. Amen!

INCREASE OUR FAITH! Luke 17:1-10

"Increase our faith!" the disciples ask Jesus in our reading. That is also our prayer today. We cry out, "Lord, increase my faith! I'm having a hard time in my life right now. I'm really struggling here." The good news today is that our faith is increased when we worship the Lord, hear his Word, and receive his gifts.

When we worship, we are reminded of God's love for lost sinners. We remember how the Father sent his Son to be our Savior. We hear the proclamation of the gospel and faith is increased. We receive the body and blood of Christ in Holy Communion, and faith grows stronger. We remember that we have been baptized in the name of the Triune God. We have received the Holy Spirit.

God does increase our faith, and he does so by the Holy Spirit. The Holy Spirit creates saving faith through the Word, Holy Baptism and the Lord's Supper. As our faith grows stronger, we are able to serve others in the way our Lord describes in our reading. We can forgive others in the same way God has forgiven us. We can begin to love and serve others in the manner Christ has loved and served us. When this happens, we become faithful servants who are only doing their duty.

We need to pray that the Lord Jesus would increase our faith because so many things can undermine our spiritual life. So many things can challenge our faith and shake our confidence in the Lord. For example, there is grief and tragedy. There is the loss of loved ones and those dear to us. There is guilt and regret over our past. There is the problem of suffering and evil. There is dealing with sickness and ongoing health problems. There is the challenge of living in a troubled world that is falling apart at the seams.

Yes, so many things can severely challenge and undermine our faith. And furthermore, there are also temptations to sin that lead us astray. Jesus said to his disciples, "Temptations to sin are sure to come, but woe to the one through whom they come. It would be better for him if a millstone were hung around his neck and he were cast into the sea."

Jesus tells us that temptations to sin are sure to come into our life. Lots of them are out there. Is our faith strong enough to withstand such temptations? Or do we find ourselves constantly giving in to sinful behavior? Is our faith weak, shaky and about to collapse? Are we struggling in our spiritual life? No wonder the apostles said, "Lord, increase our faith!" They looked at their life, and they knew that they were weak and frail sinners. They were well aware of their shortcomings and failures. And so, they cried out, "Increase our faith!"

However, notice what really prompted this request. Look again at what the disciples are specifically responding to. Jesus told them, "If your brother sins, rebuke him, and if he repents, forgive him, and if he sins against you seven times in a day, and turns to you seven times, saying, 'I repent,' you must forgive him." That is when the apostles cried out, "Increase our faith!"

It is as if they were saying, "Lord, we're not able to do all this forgiving. We don't have enough faith to cover it. This is beyond our ability to do." That is true, humanly speaking. To really forgive those who sin against us is hard to do. We find it much easier to get angry and carry a grudge. We would rather retaliate than forgive. We would rather yell and lash out.

It seems as if the Lord were asking the impossible of us here. How can he expect us to live in such forgiveness? How can we have such a faith? The surprising answer is that you already have such a faith. It has already been given to you in Holy Baptism. You are a child of God. You belong to the Father. The blood of Christ has redeemed you. You have the Holy Spirit. You have faith.

Notice when the apostles say, "Increase our faith," the Lord says, "If you had faith like a grain of mustard seed, you could say to this mulberry tree, 'Be uprooted and planted in the sea,' and it would obey you." In other words, the disciples already had faith. It might be tiny and smaller than a mustard seed, but it was there.

So really, the disciples were asking for the wrong thing. They didn't really need to increase their faith; they needed to increase their faithfulness. There is a big difference. Faith is a gift from God. Faithfulness is our response to God's gift. Faithfulness is what we do with the gift we have received. This is where we strive to serve our Lord by following his Word and putting it into practice.

When we accept Christ as our Savior, we put our faith in him. We trust that he is the one who died on the cross for us. The millstone of our sins was hung around his neck. He was cast into the sea. Our Lord carried all of our guilt; he suffered our punishment; he took all of our sins and failures and mistakes down into the depths of the sea. He suffers and dies for us. He paid the price with his shed blood.

This is why your sins are forgiven. They are truly forgiven through the cross of Jesus. This is God's gift to you. But now you are called to share the gift. You are called to be a faithful servant, a Christian who lives in God's forgiveness each day. God had forgiven you totally, absolutely and unconditionally – now you show your faith by forgiving others.

There is an old story about Thomas Edison. Edison was well known for his ability to delegate work to others. When he and his staff were developing the first light bulb, it took hundreds of hours to manufacture a single bulb. One day, after finishing one of the first prototypes, Edison handed the light bulb to a young errand boy and asked him to take it upstairs to the testing room. As the boy turned and started up the stairs, he stumbled and fell, and the bulb shattered on the steps.

Instead of yelling at the boy and lashing out, Edison reassured him that he was forgiven. He said, "Son, you made a mistake. I forgive you." Edison then turned to his staff and told them to get to work on another bulb. When it was completed several days later, Thomas Edison demonstrated the reality of his forgiveness in the most powerful way. He walked over to the same boy, handed him the light bulb, and said, "Please take this up to the testing room." Forgiveness gave that boy a second chance and a new opportunity.

That's how it is with you and God. When God forgives you, your past mistakes are gone. They are cast into the depths of the sea. You are forgiven, totally and absolutely by the grace of God. You are given a second chance and a new opportunity to serve. Our gracious God bestows absolution, and now you are called to forgive others in the same way God has forgiven you. Certainly, that's not easy to do. But we need to move beyond our excuses and rely upon the grace we have received. When the Lord says, "Okay, here is how I want you to live and treat others," we need to be faithful servants who do our Christian duty.

Remember, God empowers you through his Word, so that you might follow the way of Christ. God the Father increases your faith through the work of the Holy Spirit. The Spirit works through Word and Sacrament, so that you can overcome your doubts and all the challenges you face. You can overcome the temptations that surround you. You can have a stronger faith. You are now able to forgive others and share the gift you have received.

Finally, Jesus leaves us with a short parable that puts things into the right perspective. He tells the story of servants who do the work that has been entrusted to them. They simply do what they were supposed to do. They don't fall back on excuses. They don't expect a medal or a standing ovation. So it is for us. We are servants of Christ who have been forgiven by the grace of God. We have been given a second chance and a new opportunity to be faithful followers of the Lord Jesus Christ. Let us make the most of our opportunity and duty. Let's put our faith into practice each day. Amen!

NO MORE TEARS: John 11:17-44

A pastor tells the following story: "When I was a little boy, I hated getting my hair washed. I knew that the shampoo would burn my eyes. That was such a painful experience. I would have to keep my eyes squeezed shut to prevent any of the shampoo from getting in. Then my mother discovered something called 'No More Tears' shampoo. This was a gentler shampoo with less irritating ingredients. It was specifically designed with children in mind. No More Tears! Thanks be to God!"

Scientific studies indicate that crying is actually good for you. It helps to release emotional tension. Crying relaxes you. It calms you down. However, while crying may be beneficial for us, the circumstances that trigger it are not. That is why tears usually symbolize tragedy and suffering. We consider crying something to be avoided. Nevertheless, all of us shed tears at some point in our life. No matter who we are, all of us cry. Some may be more private than others. We may choose to not let other people see us crying, but we all shed tears. When was the last time you cried?

When was the last time you really cried tears of anguish? Perhaps it was the death of someone special. The pain was simply too great for you to bear. Perhaps it was because of some marriage or family problem. Maybe your heart was broken by someone very close to you. Perhaps you saw a news report of a tragedy or some terrorist attack. So many things can bring us grief. It can be the loss of a job or having to move. It can be financial troubles or an unsatisfying life. It can be the loneliness we experience. It can be the regret and remorse we feel over the stupid mistakes we have made in our life. It can be almost anything that brings us pain.

Wouldn't it be great if we lived in a world where tears would no longer be necessary? Wouldn't it be great if there were no more pain, sadness, or grief? Imagine living in a world where there is no more death or mourning or crying or pain. Let us now look at the story of Lazarus in John 11.

First, we see how the Son of God knows all about our tears. A dear friend of Jesus has died. John tells us that Jesus loved Lazarus and his two sisters, Martha and Mary. They were all close friends. But now, Lazarus is dead. Jewish burial customs required that a body be buried on the day of death. The body was washed, carefully anointed with perfume and spices, and then wrapped in strips of linen. After this, the body was laid in a grave or a tomb.

Lazarus has died. He has been buried. The funeral has been held. Jesus now goes to visit his friends in Bethany. But notice how he is late for Lazarus' funeral. And he wasn't just a few minutes late, or even a few hours late, but he was a few days late. It looks like Martha and Mary are hurt because Jesus was not there. They thought he could have healed their brother and prevented his death from even occurring. Now, it is too late. The one they loved so dearly has been taken away from them. Lazarus is gone. This is undoubtedly why Martha and Mary are so upset with Jesus. Why didn't he come earlier when they called him? He could have prevented all this! However, he did not arrive until days later. Why?

We often are like Martha and Mary when we experience tragedy. We also have our questions. We also ask, "Why, Lord? Why did this have to happen? Why didn't you do something to prevent all this from occurring?" We all have our questions. Martha even says to Jesus, "Lord, if you had been here, my brother would not have died." Mary says the same thing, too.

The Lord answers all of our questions with one of the greatest statements in the entire Bible. Jesus says, "I am the resurrection and the life. Whoever believes in me shall live, even though he dies. In fact, everyone who believes in me shall never die. Martha, do you believe this?" The Lord calls for us to believe in him, to believe even in the face of tragedy. We need to believe in Christ, even in the presence of death. We need to believe, even as we stand at the gravesite of a loved one.

Jesus is the true resurrection and the life. Whoever believes in him shall live forever. Even though we pass through death, we shall live with him forever in a new and better life. Do you believe this?

And let's not think that our Lord stands aloof from our pain and tears. He doesn't simply look down upon us from high above and speak pious platitudes like, "Don't worry. You'll get over it. It will be all right. Time heals all. Just move on, and you'll be fine." No, the Son of God fully enters into our pain and sorrow. Jesus is deeply troubled by this tragedy. He is deeply moved in spirit. He is always touched by our tragedy and grief. The Lord shares our sorrow. He cries our tears.

We now see how Christ goes to the tomb of his friend, Lazarus. He sees the sisters weeping in sorrow. He sees the anguish and heartache of the people gathered there. And Jesus himself weeps. He cries tears of sadness.

The Son of God fully enters into our suffering and pain. He cries our tears, and these tears remind us we never suffer alone. In Christ, God himself enters into our heartache and grief. God cries our tears. Jesus not only weeps, but he also does something about our painful situation. He tells the sisters, "Roll away the stone." And so, they open the tomb by removing the stone that sealed it.

Then, Jesus cried out in a loud voice, "Lazarus, come forth!" And the man who had been dead for four days came out, his hands and feet covered with linen strips, and his face wrapped with a cloth. Jesus then said to them, "Unbind him and let him go!" Here Christ demonstrates that he truly is the resurrection and the life. He is the Savior who gives life to the dead. He gives salvation to the lost and hope to the hopeless. And he does this by fully entering into our life and our death. The sinless Son of God will die on the cross for all of our sins. And as Christ hangs upon that cross, the women who had followed from Galilee will watch him die. They will weep their tears of sadness. They will watch their Lord suffer and finally breathe his last.

Then, they will take his bruised and battered body down from the cross and will wrap it in strips of linen. A cloth will cover his face, just like the cloth that covered the face of Lazarus. Jesus will then be quickly placed in a tomb. There will not be time on Good Friday to properly anoint his body with perfume and spices. The women will come back on Sunday morning to finish that job.

However, when they arrive at the tomb on Sunday morning, they discover that the tomb is empty. Only the strips of linen are lying there. Christ had risen from the dead, alive and victorious. This proves that Jesus truly is the resurrection and the life. And when we put our faith in him, we discover that we are now able to cope with tragedy and heartache.

The resurrection of Christ now changes everything. It fully redeems our suffering. We now discover that we can make it through those difficult times of our life. His resurrection gives us the power to keep going. His life gives us a new hope and his love reminds us that we are never alone. The Son of God has truly entered into our world and into our life. He has cried our tears. He has died our death. He gave himself so that we might live forever. This victory is yours right now, by faith. On the last day, you will fully and completely enter into it, for all time and eternity. On the last day, you will enter God's new creation.

Never forget the tremendous power of faith. When Job was in the midst of experiencing great suffering and pain, he looked to his Redeemer. Even after Job lost his family, his health, and his possessions, he could still confess, "I know that my Redeemer lives. I know that even though I die, I shall see him for myself. With my own eyes, I will behold him."

Job's faith was able to sustain him through the darkest hours of his life. Job was able to look forward to the last day and the victory that we will one day enter into. This is the victory of having our bodies raised from the dead and glorified. It is the victory of seeing God face-to-face and living in his presence forevermore. It is the victory of being reunited with our loved ones who have gone before us. The Bible tells us that on that last day, there will be no more tears.

Now that is an amazing statement! From the time of Adam and Eve, tears have been shed over death, pain, sickness, tragedy, and endless disasters. How many oceans would all those tears fill? However, according to Revelation, a time is coming when there will be no more tears. Revelation says, "On the last day, God will wipe the tears from our eyes, and there will be no more death or mourning or crying or pain. For the old order of things will have passed away. God will make all things new."

On that last day, God will renew this entire universe. In this renewed creation, we will have that perfect and complete life God intended for Adam and Eve to have in the first place. Then, there will be no more crying or pain. Then, God will wipe all our tears away forever. No more tears! Do you remember what Jesus said to Martha? "I am the resurrection and the life. Whoever believes in me shall live forever. Martha, do you believe this?"

Do you believe this? Do you truly believe that Jesus is the resurrection and the life? Do you believe that death does not have the last word? Do you believe the victory is yours? The day is coming when we will live together with Christ forever, and we shall see our loved ones again. With our own eyes, we shall behold our Redeemer and all the saints who have gone before us. Such a hope can give us strength and courage. Such a faith is a powerful thing! It fills us with a real hope and the strong confidence that better days are coming.

Here is the bottom line: In this earthly life, we will all experience tears. We all experience pain and grief. We will experience the loss of our loved ones. Today our Lord promises us a new creation where tears of sorrow will never be shed again. Here is a powerful hope that helps you to live each day with confidence and joy. You are safe in God's love. Christ has risen and he lives for you. Jesus is your resurrection and life. He is your hope. Do you believe this? Amen!

THE END OF YOUR ROPE: 1 Kings 19:1-21

What do you do when you come to the end of your rope? When the bottom is reached, when the rope runs out, when you are all alone, what then? What is beyond the end of the rope? No more rope is left. You have only another day to face. Do you ever feel like that? Do you ever feel like there is no hope and no reason to go on? Do you ever feel like just giving up?

Today we look at the prophet Elijah. He has just come off the heels of a great victory. The story is familiar. There was a great contest between Elijah and the prophets of Baal on Mount Carmel. Baal was a false god that the people of Israel had started to worship. King Ahab was a big fan of this Canaanite god. Encouraged by his wife Jezebel, Ahab led the people astray by forsaking the one true God and by advocating the worship of Baal.

Elijah confronted the prophets of Baal and challenged them to a contest on Mount Carmel. Elijah had two altars built. He then told those prophets to pray to their god Baal to come and set the sacrifice on their altar on fire. They prayed and prayed for hours. They danced around and chanted all day long, but nothing happened. Then, Elijah told the people who had assembled, "Now watch what God can do."

Elijah prayed, and fire from heaven set his altar ablaze. All the people cheered and cried out, "The Lord is God! The Lord is God!"

You would have thought the people of Israel would have regained their senses. Surely now they would follow the one true God once again. Surely now, they would return to the Lord who had rescued them from the slavery of Egypt so long ago. They would now come back to the God who had made a covenant with them at Mount Sinai. However, that was not the case.

Very soon afterward, Elijah found himself on the outside looking in. Queen Jezebel was so angry about this contest she vowed to kill Elijah that very day. The prophet of God had to flee for his life. Elijah took off, heading south as fast as he could run. Elijah learned there are no permanent victories in this life. The people had cheered for him on Mount Carmel for a day, but they quickly fell back into their old ways. They started worshipping Baal once more.

Therefore, Elijah fled down south into the wilderness of Judea. And as he did so, both his body and mind went into hiding. He went into a deep depression. He began to feel sorry for himself. The injustice was just too much. It seemed like the Lord had let him down. God had given him a great victory, but then allowed this terrible crisis to happen. His life was now in danger. He had to run away to save his skin.

And it felt like God had deserted him. Elijah felt all alone, discouraged, frustrated and afraid. He had come to the end of his rope.

This happens to us, too. Life is not fair. Things may be going well for a while, but then, everything falls apart. A sudden crisis comes and everything becomes unglued. That is when we struggle. We stumble and fall. The sun stops shining. Suddenly, all is dark. We slip into a deep depression. We come to the end of our rope.

What is beyond the end of the rope? When the bottom is reached and the rope runs out, what then? When all is dark and it seems like there is no hope, what should we do?

It was at this point that Elijah had a choice to make. The next day came and it found him sleeping under a tree. He was exhausted and out of gas. However, God sent an angel to wake him up and to feed him. This happened not just once, but twice. Then, the angel said, "Okay, Elijah. What is it going to be? Are you going to just say, NO, and continue to wallow in your self-pity? Are you going to keep running away from all your troubles? Or will you get up and say, YES? Are you going to say, YES to God, YES to life, YES to hope?"

Elijah finally got up. He arose, dusted himself off, and went down to a cave on Mount Sinai. Here, Elijah begins a dialogue with God. He told God all of his troubles and the Lord listened. God said, "Elijah, what are you doing here, inside this lonely cave?" And Elijah said, "Lord, I've reached the end of my rope. Look, I have served you faithfully, but I have to say, I feel like you let me down. Your people have forsaken your covenant; they have thrown down your altars. They have killed all your prophets. I'm the only one left, and now Jezebel is seeking my life."

The Lord said, "Okay, I hear you. Now, go stand outside. I have something to say to you." Elijah then goes outside and a great wind comes roaring by, but God was not in the wind. A great earthquake then shook the mountain, but God was not in the earthquake. A blazing fire appeared, but God was not in the great fire. Then, the sound of a gentle whisper came to Elijah. God was in that whisper and he told Elijah to go back to the land of Israel because he still had some work for him to do.

The Lord told Elijah that he knew what he was doing. He had matters well in hand. God was still in control, and he had a plan for Elijah and his people. The Lord told Elijah, "You should stop complaining so much. My grace is sufficient for you. My power is made perfect in weakness." In other words, when you reach the end of your rope, you discover that God is there. In fact, he has been there all along. What is beyond the end of the rope? God! God is there for you.

And notice how God doesn't come to Elijah in the great wind or the powerful earthquake or the roaring fire. But God comes to us in a gentle whisper. God comes in a gentle, quiet way. God speaks to us through simple words written in a book, through the plain waters of Holy Baptism, through the ordinary bread and wine of Holy Communion.

The Lord God speaks to us through Word and Sacrament. God comes to us in worship and he says, "What are you running away for? Why do you think that you are all alone and that no one cares about you? Why do you think all is lost?" God comes to us when we are at the end of our rope, and he speaks to us in a gentle, quiet whisper. God does not speak to us in a great big wind or an earthquake or fire. But he comes to us in the sound of a gentle stillness.

That is how God saved the world, through the gentle stillness of his Son dying on a cross. That happened on a dark Friday afternoon. All was quiet and still. The sun had stopped shining. Total darkness covered the land. A deep silence descended upon Golgotha. Left all alone, deserted and abandoned by all, the Son of God carries the sins of the whole world upon his soul. All alone, he bears our punishment, he suffers our anguish, and he carries our burden. Jesus reaches the end of his rope as he suffers and dies for all.

Our Lord reaches the end of his rope as he dies upon that cross. He is abandoned and forsaken, rejected and persecuted, crucified and killed. He dies and is buried. However, in the quiet stillness of an early morning a few days later, we discover the gentle whisper of an empty tomb. We discover that there is life after death. There is sunshine after darkness. There is joy after sadness. There is hope after our struggle with depression.

You see, in Christ there is victory and this is a permanent victory because this is the victory of his resurrection. It is the promise of the life of the world to come. Through the cross and resurrection of Jesus, we discover that God is with us. He is with us even as we struggle with our depression and darkness. God is with us, even as we reach the end of our rope. God is with us, even when we feel like giving up.

Here is a wondrous grace, a powerful grace that reaches out to you today. God says, "I know what you are going through. I know your pain and struggles. I know your loneliness and grief. And I care. I deeply care about you, I always have, and I always will. Never forget that. Never forget how much I love you."

God the Father says, "Remember the story of Elijah and how he struggled. Remember my Son and how he suffered for you. Also, remember that his tomb is now empty. Christ has risen and he lives for you. Never forget that I am in control of all things, and I have a plan for you and your life. I am with you always!"

Now, we are able to get up, dust ourselves off, and face another day. Now, we have the confidence and strength that God gives. Now, we get up and say, YES. We can carry on, knowing that even though we go through the ups and downs of life, the Lord is with us.

God is there for you. He will help you through those valleys of depression. With God's help, you can say, YES to another day. You can say, YES to life, YES to hope in Christ, YES to the gifts of grace God freely bestows. Amen!

LIKE A ROARING LION: 1 Peter 5:6-11

Today, the apostle Peter speaks of a lion. He says this lion has been devouring unsuspecting prey from the beginning of time and he remains on the prowl even today. This lion is the devil. His goal is to take as many of us down into hell with him as he can. Since the devil is out to get us, it would be good to know how to protect ourselves. Peter says there are three things that keep us safe: humility, self-control, and grace.

Peter first of all tells us, "Humble yourself under God's mighty hand. God will lift you up in due time. Cast all your anxieties upon him because he cares for you." Peter says, "Humble yourself." This means we repent of our sins. We confess that we need God's help here. We are sinners. We admit that we need God's mercy and grace.

We humble ourselves, and then God lifts us up with that word of absolution, "Your sins are forgiven!" God declares, "For the sake of my Son, Jesus Christ, your sins are taken away!" This word of grace lifts up our hearts and restores our soul.

To humble yourself before the Lord God also means that you surrender all your cares and worries unto him. Remember, the devil likes to use our worries to get us to second-guess and doubt God. The devil loves to see us anxious and fearful about the future. That word "anxiety" is used this way in the story of Mary and Martha. Do you remember how Martha invited Jesus and his disciples over for dinner?

Mary sat at Jesus' feet while Martha fussed and worried about whether there would be enough food for everyone to eat. Martha was doing all the work while her sister was listening to Jesus teach. Martha ended up getting all worked up. In fact, she got so angry that went over to Jesus and started yelling at him. "Don't you even care that my sister has left me to do all the work? Tell her to do something!" Jesus then said to her, "Martha, you are anxious and worried about many things. But Mary has chosen what is better."

That is how the devil works. He loves to create anxiety and worry in our life. Often, we are just like Martha. We are so busy with household chores, work, sports, school, or family commitments. We have so many things going on in our life. We feel overwhelmed. We get all anxious and upset. And we end up like Martha, full of anger and accusations, yelling at the Lord, blaming him for all of our woes.

The devil loves to get us started down this path. If you see this happening in your life, humble yourself under God's mighty hand.

Cast all your anxiety on him. There is no better place to take your worries and fears. God loves you and has promised to care for you. Peter says, "Take every care and concern and worry you have, and give them all to the Lord to carry. Cast all your anxieties on him because he cares for you." In other words, humble yourself before God. Let the Lord bear your burdens. Let him lead you through life each day. Let go of your anxiety and anger and give it all to the Lord.

Now, as you cast all of your burdens on God, it is important that you do not become lulled into a false sense of security, thinking that now the danger of attack has passed. The devil will not give up so easily. You need to remain alert. Peter now tells us, "Be self-controlled and alert. Remember, your enemy the devil prowls around like a roaring lion looking for someone to devour. Resist him by standing firm in the faith." To be "self-controlled" means we avoid temptation. We turn away from what is sinful and wrong. We stay away from what could spiritually hurt us. We don't lose control and give in to the devil's temptation. We don't want to foolishly enter into the lion's cage and pull on his tail. That is asking for trouble.

However, sometimes we do just that. We allow ourselves to be seduced by what we know is wrong and sinful. We give in to temptation and sin against God and break his commandments. That is when we end up getting hurt. We feel lousy and full of guilt and remorse. Endless regret eats us up inside. It is best to be sober-minded and self-controlled, and to be watchful and alert. We need to repent of our sins and turn away from anything that could hurt us. Resist the devil by rejecting the temptations he offers. Resist him by standing firm in the faith. Follow the Word of God, and live each day in the Word. God's Word is powerful.

Our Lord Jesus proved that God's Word could topple the devil. When Jesus was tempted by the devil for 40 days in the wilderness, he answered him with Holy Scripture. Therefore, arm yourself with God's Word. Memorize Bible verses so that you can make quick use of them when the devil attacks. Remember the Word of God and hold fast to God's promises. Be in the Word every day. Read the Bible and let the Holy Spirit speak to your heart.

While humility and self-control will prepare us for those attacks by the devil, it is only God's grace that will bring us through in the end. God's grace is the key to receiving the final victory. Remember, our God is a God of grace. He is the God of mercy and compassion. He picks us up when we fall. He forgives us when we sin. Listen again to the promise Peter extends to us: "And the God of grace who called you to glory in Christ, after you have suffered a little while, will himself restore you. God will make you strong, firm and steadfast."

When you fall, turn to the Lord Jesus for forgiveness. Christ has defeated the devil by refusing to fall for any of his tricks. Christ undid the devil's handiwork by taking upon himself the punishment of hell we deserved. Jesus carried our burden. He suffered and died to pay the penalty we owed. He died and rose again for you. That is why, in Christ, you are victorious over the devil. God's grace in Christ makes you to be strong, firm and steadfast.

Can you imagine how disappointed the devil must have been at our Lord's resurrection? The devil thought he had totally defeated God's Son. However, in reality, he was the one who was defeated and beaten. Our Lord rose from the dead, alive and victorious. Christ has now totally defeated sin, death and the power of the devil.

Therefore, here is the bottom line. Since the devil could not defeat our Lord, he has now gone to plan "B," which is attacking us. The devil does not want you to believe that Jesus has won forgiveness for you. He doesn't want you to believe that you can have a new life through his resurrection. He doesn't want you to know that God loves you and cares for you each day.

The devil is still out there, right now. He is prowling around like a roaring lion, looking for someone to devour. So stay alert and be self-controlled. Do not let that lion take a bite out of you. Stay close to the Lord Jesus and you will be safe. Humble yourself under God's mighty hand and he will lift you up. Cast all of your cares on him, for he cares for you.

Trust that God is in control, no matter what you encounter. Remain watchful, standing firm in the faith, armed with the powerful Word of God. Pray every day in the Spirit. And the God of grace who has called you to eternal glory will keep you safe, through faith in Jesus Christ. To him be the glory, power and honor, forever and ever. Amen!

THE LORD IS MY SHEPHERD: Psalm 23:1-6

A shepherd had 100 sheep in his flock. One evening, he counted them as they came back home through the gate of the sheep pen. Only 99 were there! One was missing. It must have been separated from the flock and become lost in the woods. At once, the shepherd closed the gate and left his helpers to watch over the flock. He had to find that lost sheep before some wolf could get to her. He hurried back to the places where the flock had been that day. He called the sheep's name repeatedly. For a while, the shepherd heard nothing. Again and again, he called. At last, he heard a weak cry. Before long, he found the sheep, all tangled up in some bushes. He gently pulled her out, but found she could not walk. She had hurt her leg. Therefore, he picked her up, and carried her home in his arms.

This shepherd is someone we all know. It is our Lord Jesus Christ. We are his sheep, and sometimes we get lost, too. We get separated from God's flock. We go down the wrong path. We get confused and lose our way. We get hurt. But today our loving Shepherd calls us back. He searches for us and calls us by name. He finds us and binds up our wounds. And this Shepherd rejoices over all his sheep.

That is what makes Psalm 23 so powerful and special. Psalm 23 is the most beloved of all the Psalms. And it begins by saying, "The Lord is my Shepherd; I shall not want." That is quite a statement, isn't it? Think about it. Our Psalm is actually saying, "Since the Lord is my Shepherd, I will never lack a thing in my life. I shall not want."

How can that be true? It often feels like there are many things lacking in our life. It often seems like we do suffer want. Our life feels empty and hollow. There is so much that is missing in our life. How can Psalm 23 say such a thing? But perhaps what is missing in our life is faith. We lack a simple trust in God's goodness and grace. That's why our faith is so shaky and uncertain. Such a lack of faith leads to endless doubts and fears.

We have such a hard time believing what God says. That is why we struggle so much in our spiritual life. It might even reach a point where we cry out, "Lord, help me! Increase my faith! Help me to trust in you. Show me how to get rid of my doubts and fears."

Today, the Shepherd calls out to his lost and foolish sheep. He says to us, "I am the Good Shepherd. I know my sheep and my sheep know me. And I lay down my life for my sheep." Our Shepherd knows us and he knows our situation. He knows our faith is weak and uncertain. The Shepherd is well aware of the condition of all of his sheep. And he knows that we are hurting inside. We feel lost and all alone.

That is why he says, "Listen to my voice when I call to you. Hear my Word! Listen to what I say and you will have all that you need." Our Shepherd wants to lead us to the green pastures of his Word. He wants to bring us once again to the still waters of Holy Baptism. He seeks to restore our soul through the power of Holy Communion.

Today, our Lord leads us down the path of his cross and resurrection. He forgives our sins for his name's sake. He anoints our head with the oil of grace. Our cup of blessing just overflows, and we once again discover what we really need in this life. Our Shepherd feeds us with his Word and Sacraments. That is why worship is so important. At worship, we hear the voice of the Shepherd who searches for us. He calls to us. He feeds our hungry heart. He restores our soul. He bestows his gift of forgiveness.

The Lord nourishes us through his Word and Sacraments, and in this way, faith is created and strengthened. Our spiritual hunger is satisfied. Our doubts and fears now begin to fade away. We receive a spiritual healing. Our wounds are bound up and we are restored. Jesus says, "I am the Good Shepherd. My sheep listen to my voice. I know them and they follow me. I give them eternal life. And my sheep shall never perish; no one can snatch them out of my hand."

Our Shepherd promises to guide us through this life. He goes ahead of us and protects us every step of the way. He says, "Come, follow me! I will show you the way to go." When the Lord steps into your life, you discover that you do have everything you need. Now, you can joyfully confess, "The Lord Jesus Christ is my shepherd; I shall not want. He makes me lie down in green pastures. He leads me beside the still waters. He restores my soul; he leads me in the paths of righteousness for his name's sake. Even though I walk through the valley of the shadow of death, I will fear no evil; for you, O Lord Jesus, are with me, your rod and staff they comfort me."

Yes, even if we walk through the deepest valley, we have everything we need. Even in the darkest of times, Christ is with us. You are safe in the loving arms of the Good Shepherd. That is important to remember when you go through those tough times. Life is often filled with the dark valleys, low points, and difficult days. We all struggle with our pain and hurts. We all experience depression, sadness and grief. Perhaps you are going through such a deep, dark valley right now in your life.

"But even if I walk through the valley of the shadow of death, I will fear no evil; for the

Lord Jesus Christ is with me. His cross and resurrection, they comfort me. In times of trouble, I turn to my Savior. The Lord is my Shepherd; I shall not want!" Always remember this: Christ laid down his life for you. That's how much he loves you. Christ was thinking of you when he died on that cross. He was thinking of you when he laid down his life. That's why you belong to him. You are his sheep, his lamb.

The Good Shepherd now calls to you. Can you hear him? He is saying, "Come on and follow me! I will walk with you through those valleys that lie ahead. Together, we can make it. I will bless you with my presence. I will feed you with my Word and Sacraments. I will strengthen your faith and give you all you need." That is the promise that the Lord Jesus makes to all of us. He gives us his Word. He prepares the table of his Supper for us. He anoints our head with the oil of baptismal grace. Our cup of blessing just overflows!

We now have that certainty of knowing that God's goodness and mercy will follow us all the days of our life. The Good Shepherd leads us through our earthly journey, and then, he leads us all the way home, where we shall dwell in the house of the Lord forever. Amen!

A CAREER CHANGE: Matthew 3:13-17

The Bible doesn't tell us much about the childhood and early years of Jesus. Our Lord's public ministry did not begin until he was about 30 years old. Until then, he was a carpenter by trade. Joseph, the stepfather of Jesus, was a carpenter. Back in those days, the father taught his son his trade. Therefore, we can guess that Jesus was a carpenter for at least 15 years. But now, a career change is in order. Jesus now moves from the business of his stepfather to the business of his heavenly Father. He will trade in his carpenter tools and become a rebuilder of God's creation.

Can you visualize Jesus as he stands in his carpenter's shop for the very last time? Can you picture him putting his tools away, clearing the workbench and sweeping up the sawdust on the floor? Can you see him standing there in the doorway of his shop for the last time?

Think of all the years Jesus spent in that carpenter's shop. Think of all the things Jesus fixed and all the projects he worked on, all the things he made. But now, it is time to begin a new project. It's time for a career change. Our Lord's journey out of the carpenter's shop will take him to the banks of the Jordan River.

There, standing in the water, is John the Baptist. He is a striking figure, dressed in camel skins with a leather belt around his waist.

John's message was, "Repent, for the kingdom of heaven is at hand!" John baptized the people for the forgiveness of sins. He was sent by God to prepare the way for the Messiah. Huge crowds of people came to him. And now, here comes Jesus of Nazareth. He wants to be baptized, too. John hesitates. In fact, John tries to prevent this from even happening. John says to Jesus, "Look, I need to be baptized by you. Why do you come to me?" But Jesus says, "Let's do this. It is fitting for us to fulfill and complete all righteousness."

In effect, Christ is saying, "This is all a part of God's plan. It is fitting that I undergo what everyone else is experiencing. I will now take my place among sinners. I completely identify myself with those whom I have come to save."

Notice how John picked up on the fact that Jesus did not need to be baptized. He had no sins to wash away. He did not need to repent. And yet, the Sinless One takes his place alongside sinners. Christ is numbered with the transgressors. He stands shoulder-to-shoulder with us in every way. Now, we see how Jesus officially begins his new career. This is the beginning of something totally new. He is baptized by John in the waters of the Jordan River.

As Jesus came up out of the water, the heavens were opened. And he saw the Spirit of God descending like a dove and coming to rest on him. Then, a voice from heaven declared, "This is my beloved Son. With him, I am well pleased." Can you picture the scene? Can you visualize the Holy Spirit descending in the form of a dove? Can you hear the soft flutter of the wings? Do you hear the booming voice from heaven, echoing across the river valley? "This is my beloved Son! With him, I am well pleased."

In the words of Isaiah, the Father declares, "This is my Son, my chosen one. This is my Servant in whom I delight. I have put my Spirit on him and he will bring salvation to the whole world. A bruised reed he will not break. A faintly burning wick he will not snuff out. He will fulfill all righteousness. Therefore, with him, I am well pleased."

Why is the heavenly Father so pleased with his Son? Perhaps it was the same pleasure Joseph felt when his young son declared that he wanted to be a carpenter, just like his dad. Perhaps it was the pleasure of having a son who is eager to learn your trade, a son who will follow your instructions and excel at his work. Jesus certainly went to work after his baptism. Now began the work of bringing salvation to the lost. Christ would now begin three years of non-stop work. He would preach and teach; he would heal the sick and raise the dead; he would feed the crowds and rescue those trapped by their sins.

Christ would travel up and down the entire land of Israel. He would fulfill all righteousness. He would carry out the Father's instructions and excel at his work. It would all culminate in what Jesus later called, "the baptism I have to undergo." This would be the baptism of the cross, that complete immersion into the penalty of sin. On the cross, Jesus would finish the work he was given to do.

That wooden cross was much like the rough wood that Jesus the carpenter had turned into beautiful furniture or fine household items. However, on the rough wood of the cross, nothing beautiful would hang. There would only be a broken body, someone wounded and dying.

But this death on the cross would complete our Lord's work. It would be the climax of his career. It would fulfill all righteousness. The Son of God would complete his mission as he is numbered with the transgressors. He would take his place among sinners in the fullest sense. Jesus completely immerses himself into our sin and guilt. "God made him who had no sin, to be sin for us, so that in him, we might become the righteousness of God." And, think about this - when Jesus died on the cross, the Father could well have once more declared, "This is my beloved Son! With him, I am well pleased." The Father could well have said, "Good job, Son! I am so proud of you. Nice work! You did a great job."

Now, this is where it gets interesting. When Jesus was baptized, he left behind his carpenter's shop for a new career. Baptism made the switch complete. After Jesus is baptized, he never looked back. Something new began. God's work and God's mission now took center stage. And the same is true for us.

When we were baptized, we were connected to the death of Jesus on that cross. We died with him, and then, we were raised from the dead, through his resurrection. Paul says, "We were buried with Christ through baptism. This happened, so that just as Christ was raised from the dead, we too, might walk in newness of life."

Baptism does bring newness. It brings a new life, a new beginning. We are born again by the water and the Word, born again by the Holy Spirit who descends upon us like a dove. Like Jesus, we are baptized and we begin our second career, so to speak. We make a career change as we begin our true vocation. We are now God's servants, God's people. The heavenly Father puts his name upon us, and we now belong to him.

Back in the days of the old west, a little girl lived in a small town on the prairies of North Texas. One Sunday morning, the little girl was baptized in her church. The next day at school, her friends asked her to describe that experience. She said, "I was a little maverick out on the prairie. But when I was baptized, God put his mark on me, and now, I belong to him!"

The word "maverick" was originally a man's name. Samuel Maverick was a Texas cattleman who, for some reason, refused to brand his cattle. Because of that, any unbranded animal that became lost came to be known as a maverick. Such a lost and straying maverick became the legal property of anyone who found it.

When we were born into this world, we were spiritual mavericks. We were lost and straying far outside the boundaries of God's ranch, far from the Father's homestead. But the Father has called to us through his Son who came to seek and save those who were lost. The Holy Spirit has brought us back into God's family through our baptism. We are now no longer mavericks, but now we belong to the Lord. We have been marked with the sign of the cross both upon our forehead and upon the heart. This shows we belong to our Father. The Holy Spirit has descended upon us, and we have heard that voice from heaven declaring,

"You are my beloved child! With you, I am well pleased."

Today, God the Father speaks that word of grace to each of us. And today, God declares that it is time for a career change. It's time to start a new chapter in your life. It's time to live as a child of God and to walk in newness of life. It's time for all of us to repent and believe the Gospel. It's time to love God and to love others.

That is our true vocation. We are called to be God's people, people who live in love and who rejoice in the gifts God freely gives. We are God's servants, people who live out their baptism every day. We are Christians, people who are willing to love and serve others and help them in their time of need.

Therefore, let us dedicate ourselves to our heavenly Father's work and to carry out the mission he has given us. There is no looking back as we begin our new career of following Jesus every day and walking in his light. Let us serve others and do the work God has given us to do. Share the gift you have received. Fulfill your baptismal calling. Always remember you are God's child! You are special in his eyes. Go now in peace and serve the Lord. Amen!

SUPERNATURAL! John 20:19-31

"The Easter story is nothing but a myth!" That is what a college professor announced to his class a few days before spring break. "Jesus did not rise from the dead. In fact, there is no God in heaven that sent his Son into this world in the first place." One student raised his hand, and said, "I believe in God." "You can believe whatever you want to," the teacher answered. "But you have to realize that the real world excludes the possibility of miracles. Miracles are scientifically impossible! Furthermore, we have no need for an Almighty God who goes around working miracles. The supernatural does not exist."

Now, I have to say, I think that is a great quote: "The supernatural does not exist." That really defines the issue for us in a clear-cut way. That is the real question before us today: "Do you believe in the supernatural? Do you believe in an Almighty God who can work miracles? Do you believe that Jesus literally rose from the dead?"

The modern world has apparently given up on the idea of God. People today do not believe in a God who is able to work miracles. They do not believe that God is able to do things way beyond our normal experience. Many people today, like this college professor, deny that God exists, and they attack Christianity whenever they get the chance. "The supernatural does not exist!" I know many people who doubt the reality of miracles, especially the resurrection of Christ. They have a hard time believing what the Bible plainly teaches.

However, this is nothing new. On that first Easter, many years ago, one of the disciples refused to believe in the resurrection of Jesus. Thomas had his doubts. He was a skeptic, like so many today. On that first Easter night, the disciples were together in a house, hiding behind locked doors. They were scared and worried that they might be arrested next.

Suddenly, Jesus stands in the middle of the room, and he says, "Peace be with you." He showed them his hands and side to prove he was the same Jesus they had known, the same guy who was crucified just three days earlier.

Now Thomas was not there when this happened. Later, when the disciples told him that Jesus had appeared to them, Thomas would not believe it. He said, "Unless I see the nail marks in his hands, and put my finger where the nails were, and put my hand into his side, I will never believe." You cannot get much more skeptical than that. "I will not believe unless I see visible proof, and reach out and touch with my own hands."

Why does Thomas refuse to believe like this? Why does he have such a stubborn unbelief? Because Thomas thought he knew better. After all, dead is dead and that is that. End of story. Dead people who are buried don't just jump up out of the grave and walk away. That is not possible, right? And this is how so many people think of the resurrection of Jesus today. Nice idea, but it didn't really happen. And even many of us get caught up in this way of thinking. We have a hard time believing in the supernatural. Many of us live in a sea of doubt. And when you're swimming in doubt, it's hard not to get wet. Doubt kind of seeps into your whole way of thinking.

Have you ever doubted? Have you ever wondered about this whole business of Jesus and the cross and resurrection? Have you ever wondered if the Christian faith is really just a myth? Have you ever doubted whether the Bible is literally true? Are you sometimes skeptical, like Thomas?

How can we get rid of such doubts? How can we know the Bible is really true? To be honest, there is nothing we can do here. There is no cure on the market that will take away all of our doubts. There is no quick fix or easy answers. Only one thing can take away our doubts. That one thing happened to Thomas one week later. On the next Sunday after Easter, the disciples were together again, and Thomas was with them this time. The doors were again locked. Suddenly, Jesus was standing in the middle of the room. "Peace be with you," he says once more. Then, Jesus focuses squarely on Thomas and invites him to do what he said he wanted to do. He invites Thomas to reach out and touch all the wounds he had sustained on the cross. "Go right ahead and touch me, Thomas. Stop your doubting and begin to believe."

This is what cured Thomas of his doubt. Even without touching Christ, he suddenly cries out, "My Lord and my God!" Thomas now becomes a man of faith, someone who believed in Christ. Thomas now knew that here was something not explainable by the known laws of nature or science. Here was God in the flesh, the risen Lord. Here was a miracle of God's power, the supernatural on display for all to see, believe, touch, and feel.

The only way to get rid of your doubts is to encounter the risen Christ as Thomas did. When the risen Lord steps into your life, you become a different person. You are changed by God's awesome power. You become filled with faith and hope. You begin to believe in the supernatural power of the Almighty God who can do all things. "With God, nothing is impossible."

"Now wait a second," you say, "Jesus literally appeared to Thomas way back then. How am I supposed to encounter Jesus today?" Okay, fair enough, but realize this: Today Jesus comes to us through his Word and Sacraments. Every time you read or hear the Word of God, the Lord stands in the middle of your life, and he says, "Peace be with you." Every time you receive the Lord's Supper, Jesus is right there, saying, "This is my body given for you. This is my blood shed for the forgiveness of your sins."

Through his Word and Sacraments, the risen Savior chases away our doubts. He fills us with faith and hope and trust in him. Every time you worship the Lord, the Holy Spirit is at work. Faith is created and sustained. You are now able to believe because God's great power is at work inside of you. That is the Holy Spirit's job. The Spirit works in a supernatural way to bring you to saving faith, and to keep you in that faith. This, in itself, is a tremendous miracle that God works in us. "With God, all things are possible."

Going back to where we started with our unbelieving college professor, let me just say that I am quite familiar with what the atheists teach. I know the modern world rejects God, and it ridicules those who believe in a supernatural God who works miracles. I know what atheists believe. In the same way, I am well aware of the laws of nature. I've studied science, too. I know all about the laws of nature and science, the laws of physics and chemistry. But I also know a God who can do all things. I know an amazing God whose power is infinite and almighty. And if God wants to, he can go above and beyond the normal laws of nature to work a miracle. (Remember, God created these laws of science and nature in the first place. God created the laws of physics and chemistry.)

Furthermore, can I really tell God what he can or cannot do? If God wants to work a miracle, can I stop him? Can I tell him, "Hey, wait a minute, don't you know the supernatural is not possible? You can't work miracles and you can't raise the dead." And concerning what the atheists teach, let me just say that I would rather believe what God teaches. I would rather put my faith in the Word of God than in some theory or idea created by a human. (Humans make mistakes all the time. God doesn't.) I would rather put my faith in a supernatural God who loves me, a God who sent his own Son to suffer and die for me. I'd rather believe in a gracious God who wants me to live with him forever. I would rather believe in the Easter resurrection of Christ.

Listen to what the Lord says to Thomas, "Because you have seen me, you have believed. Blessed are those who have not seen me and yet have believed." Jesus is here talking about you and me. We have not seen the risen Lord with our own eyes like Thomas did. But we believe, and we believe because the risen Lord now comes to us through his Word and Sacraments. John tells us, "Jesus did many other miraculous signs that are not recorded in this Gospel. But these are written that you may believe that he is the Christ, the true Son of God, and that by believing in him, you may have life in his name."

Think about that. All these miracles that John, Thomas, and the other disciples witnessed were written down, so that you might believe in Christ as your Savior. John says, "I wrote down these events and miracles that Jesus did, so that you may believe our testimony that he really is the promised Messiah."

That is why it's so important to read the written Word of God. Read the Gospel of John and study it. Be in the Word and worship the Lord. Receive God's gifts. Take the Lord's Supper in repentance and faith, live out our Baptism every day, and put your faith into action. When you do all this, Jesus will speak to your heart, just as he spoke to Thomas so long ago. He will take away your doubts. The Holy Spirit will change you into someone who believes. You will be transformed into someone who has a living and powerful and active faith.

God's light will shine upon you as you become convinced of his truth and the reality of his power. The Holy Spirit will bring certainty and conviction into your spiritual life. But the key here is to actually pick up the Bible and read it every day. Begin with the Gospel of John. Then, read Romans. Then, work your way through the Book of Psalms. Continue on with your readings as God leads you. If you don't understand something, move on and keep going. You can go back later and explore something that puzzled you, using a study guide or commentary. When you read the Bible with an open mind, you will discover an all-powerful God who can do all things. God can work supernatural miracles, and he can fill your soul with joy and peace.

Peter says, "Though you have not seen Christ, you love him. And even though you do not see him now, you believe in him and are filled with an inexpressible and glorious joy, for you are receiving the goal of your faith, the salvation of our souls." Discover the truth and beauty of God's Word. Then, you will discover the risen Christ who says, "Peace be with you!" You will experience the power of the Holy Spirit, and will joyfully confess, along with Thomas and all the disciples, "My Lord and my God!" Amen!

A LESSON IN GIVING: Mark 12:38-44

A man came to a Lutheran Church and asked to see the pastor. "Pastor," he said, "My dog died and I would like for you to give him a Christian burial." The pastor said, "I'm sorry to hear about your dog, but we Lutherans don't do funerals for dogs. You might try the Congregational church down the street." The man said, "I'm sorry you won't do my dog's funeral, but I understand. However, I was wondering, how much do you think is appropriate to leave as a memorial? I was thinking of giving $1,000 in honor of my dog." "Now wait a minute!" the pastor said. "You didn't tell me that your dog was a Lutheran!"

Money talks. It always gets our attention. It certainly got attention that day long ago when Jesus visited the temple in Jerusalem. Mark says that Jesus sat down opposite the temple treasury and watched the people putting money into the offering bins. These were 12 large horn-shaped metal receptacles. The people would come by and toss their money into the metal horns. They didn't have paper money back then. They had large and small coins. The large coins would make more noise than the small ones. And many coins thrown in sounded much better than just a few. People back then weren't dummies. They had figured out that if you want to really impress someone, throw in lots of large coins. And that is what the people were doing the day when Jesus visited the temple.

But then Jesus heard two faint little clinks. A widow had just thrown in two little coins that weren't worth a lot of money, just a couple of pennies. However, this really caught the Lord's attention. He said, "This woman gave more than all the rest because she gave all she had." Here was a vivid demonstration of a powerful faith in God's promises. This widow didn't have a lot of money, but she gave all that she had. She held nothing back. She gave all. Why?

Why would she give everything she had to God? She did that because God was everything to her. She had no husband to provide for her. No job to sustain her. No Social Security or retirement accounts to fall back on. All she had was God. And to show her gratitude to the Lord, she gave it all back to him.

Today, the widow in the temple gives us a lesson in giving. The first lesson we learn is that giving is an act of faith; it is our act of worship. Giving helps us to confess that God is everything to us. We confess that God is number one; God is first in our life. And we confess we need his help to see us through. Therefore, we completely trust that God will take care of us. However, can we really trust

God in such an absolute and total way? That is what our story from Mark boils down to. Can we believe what God says to us in his Word?

Can I really trust God? Can I trust God, when my life falls apart? Can I trust God, when I lose my job? Can I trust God, when my health fails me? Can I really trust God, when I breathe my last breath and die?

There are so many promises in the Bible where the Lord invites us to take him at his Word. We are called to be like the widow in the temple who gave to God because she totally relied upon the Lord.

For example, God says in Malachi, "Bring the full tithe into my storehouse. Put me to the test and see if I do not open the windows of heaven for you and pour down overflowing blessings." You see, God promises to take care of us and to provide an overflowing blessing when we give to him. But do we really believe this?

Giving is always an act of faith. It gets right to the heart of what we believe. The poor woman at the temple had nothing but God, and God was enough for her. Her giving showed this. Her actions demonstrated her faith. She trusted in God's promises and her giving demonstrated this. There is something else giving teaches us. Giving helps us to overcome our innate selfishness. It helps us to rise above thinking only about ourselves. It leads us to think about others and how we can help them.

We can stop being so self-centered all the time. This is our second point.

The story is told of a member of a church who was very wealthy. He was a rich man, but he had never been known for his generosity. The church was involved in a big building program and some members decided to pay this man a visit. When they met with him one afternoon, they said, "Sir, in view of your considerable resources and assets, would you like to make a contribution to our building program?"

The man said, "Not so fast! Did you know that I have a widowed mother who has no means of support?" "No," they responded, "We didn't know that." "Did you know that I have a sister with five children who was left by her husband, and she has no means to provide for them?" "No," they said, "We didn't know that either."

"Did you know that I have a brother who was injured by an automobile accident and can never work another day in his life? He has no way to support his wife and family." Embarrassed, they responded, "No sir, we did not know that either." "Well then," he said, "I've never given any of them a red cent, so why should I give anything to you?"

"Why should I give anything to you?" That is exactly our second point. Giving helps us to overcome our sinful, selfish nature. It helps us to remember that God is the giver of all good gifts. Everything we have is a gift. Our life is a gift, our health is a gift, our family is a gift, our assets and possessions are a gift from God. We brought nothing into this world and we take nothing with us when we die. Everything belongs to God, and we should use our possessions to help others and to serve them.

Remember that God has given us the greatest gift of all, his Son. God the Father loved this world so much that he gave his Son for us. In Jesus Christ, we see the Savior who gave everything for us. He came to help others and serve them, and Christ held nothing back. But he gave all, totally and absolutely, for us and our salvation.

It was Jesus himself who said, "It is more blessed to give than to receive." Now stop and think about that for a moment. "It is more blessed to give than to receive." Here is our lesson in giving. Jesus shows us the way of his cross and empty tomb. He shows us that when we give, we follow the way of the Messiah. He gave himself totally for us; therefore, we now give ourselves totally to him. "It is more blessed to give than to receive." Such a giving helps us to remember that everything belongs to God. He is the Creator of all things. We have been entrusted with our possessions. We now use our wealth to serve the Lord and to help others.

We are stewards who have been given a trust. Jesus says, "From everyone who has been given much, much will be required. From the one who has been entrusted with much, much will be asked." We have been given much. We have been so richly blessed. We have received salvation as a free gift from God. We have received life and health, house and home, food and clothing. God has given to each of us so many blessings. We are servants who have been entrusted with much.

As faithful stewards, we now serve our Lord through our gifts and offerings. Giving is our act of worship, our act of praise. When we give, we know that God will provide. Our heavenly Father will bless us according to his good and gracious will. He will continue to provide for us tomorrow, even as he has in the past.

Moreover, just like the widow in the temple who gave all she had, we totally give ourselves to the Lord. We know that Jesus totally gave himself for us. We know that he loves us and watches over us every day. Therefore, we can rest secure in his promises and grace. That is why we can now give to God, joyfully and freely. We have learned our lesson in giving and we have learned it well. Amen!

THE SON SETS YOU FREE: John 8:31-36

In an old "Peanuts" comic strip, there was a conversation between Lucy and Charlie Brown. Lucy was in a philosophical mood. She says, "Life is like a deck chair on a cruise ship. Some people place their chairs looking forward, so that they can see where they are going. Some place them looking back, so that they can see where they have been. That's how people are." Charlie Brown replied, "I can't even get my chair unfolded!"

Today, we look back at Martin Luther and the Reformation. We look back so that we can appreciate what we have today. We also look forward to the future in faith. We rejoice that we are free to worship God with joy and gladness. We are free to leave the past behind and look forward in faith.

Today, our Lord Jesus talks about freedom. Jesus says, "If you abide in my Word, you are truly my disciples. Then, you will know the truth and the truth will set you free." When the people in the crowd heard this, they were highly offended. They thought they didn't need to be made free. They weren't slaves to anyone. They had all the freedom they needed.

But, Jesus plainly says, "I tell you the truth, everyone who commits sin is a slave to sin."

To be honest, we also don't like hearing this. No one likes to be reminded that we are slaves to sin. We would rather deny that sin has such a firm grip upon us. However, the truth is we are trapped in the worst kind of slavery, which we can never break.

We are addicted to sin. Like an alcoholic, we are trapped, boxed-in, and stuck in our old ways. Our sinful desires continually lead us astray. The temptations we face are just too powerful. It is too easy for us to sin and fall away from God. In spite of our firm resolve to change our ways, our bondage to sin is never quite broken. And our denial that we are slaves is just further proof we are hopelessly trapped. We cannot do anything to free ourselves.

In the sixteenth century, Martin Luther found himself in a church that had an elaborate system for offering people personal freedom. Freedom could be obtained if you confessed all of your sins to a priest, and then did a series of good works that would make satisfaction for your guilt. In this way, you could secure for yourself the forgiveness of sins.

However, one big problem was that even while you were doing these good works of satisfaction, you were already committing new sins, which now had to be confessed and paid for. You soon found yourself on an endless treadmill of guilt and condemnation.

As an Augustinian monk, Luther tried to find spiritual peace by observing all the rules and regulations of monastic life. He did everything required. But the more works Luther did, the less freedom he experienced.

The church of Luther's day had made the forgiveness of sins an endless series of hoops you had to jump through. And you could never be sure if you had jumped through enough hoops to satisfy God. You can never be certain if your sins really were forgiven or not. You were kind of stuck in your guilt and moral failings.

What Jesus says today brings us sweet relief. He says, "If the Son sets you free, you will be free indeed." Here is our hope! The Son of God does what we could never do on our own. He sets us free from our guilt and failures. He releases us from the condemnation of the law.

Paul says, "For there is no distinction: For all have sinned and fall short of the glory of God, and are justified by God's grace as a free gift. This comes only through the redemption that is in Christ Jesus, whom God the Father put forward as a propitiation by his blood, to be received by faith."

You can't free yourself. Only the Son of God has the power and authority to set you free. The Son of God wins this freedom by becoming a slave in our place. He humbles himself and becomes our servant. He becomes a slave to sin as he dies on the cross. He enters our slavery as he bears our burden and suffers that punishment we merit. He is the "propitiation by blood."

This means that Jesus paid the price for our rebellion against God. He made satisfaction for the sins of the whole world. He shed his blood for us on Good Friday. Therefore, the price has been paid in full. There is no need for us to add anything. "It is finished," our Lord cried out from the cross.

You can't free yourself. Only Jesus can set you free. This is exactly what Martin Luther discovered. We are saved by grace through faith in Jesus Christ. We are saved by faith, apart from any works of satisfaction. Christ has paid the price. You are set free from sin and guilt. And if the Son sets you free, you will be free indeed!

Salvation is a gift of God's undeserved grace. We receive this gift by faith. We are justified by faith apart from works of the law. We put our faith in our Lord's work of atonement and we discover that we are now set free. Listen: Christ has made propitiation by his blood. You are forgiven! You are now set free to live for God. Your sins are forgiven and gone forever.

Luther summarizes this so well when he says in his Small Catechism, "I believe that Jesus Christ, true God, begotten of the Father from eternity, and also true man, born of the Virgin Mary, is my Lord. He has redeemed me, a lost and condemned person, purchased and won me from all sins, from death, and from the power of the devil. Not with gold or silver, but with his holy, precious blood and with his innocent suffering and death, so that I may be his own and live under him in his kingdom and serve him in everlasting righteousness, innocence, and blessedness, just as he is risen from the dead, lives and reigns to all eternity. This is most certainly true."

That is the very core and center of the entire Bible. This is God's message to all people: Jesus Christ has rescued us from our slavery to sin. The power of death and the devil has been broken forever. Our Lord shed his holy and precious blood so that we might be his own forever. We now belong to him. We live under Christ in his kingdom of grace.

Now here is something else Martin Luther discovered through his study of the Scriptures. Even though we are truly forgiven and set free, we still have our sinful nature to contend with. Even though we are Christians, we still are sinners. We are saints and sinners at the same time. However, our addiction to sin has been broken, and our job now is to be true disciples of Christ with the help of the Holy Spirit.

You might say, we are "recovering sinners" who seek to hang on to our newfound "sobriety." We repent where necessary and resolve to amend what is wrong in our life through the power of God. We seek to abide in the Word of Christ and stay sober. We are disciples of the risen Lord who follow his way and rejoice in his truth. We now want to "serve him in everlasting righteousness, innocence, and blessedness."

Finally, here is also another dimension to our freedom that we don't appreciate enough. For some reason, we have a hard time applying this truth to ourselves. Here is something every one of us struggles with. We know that God has forgiven us. For the sake of Christ, God has forgiven all your sins and he remembers them no more. They are forgiven and forgotten, thrown into the depths of the sea. We all know that.

But somehow or another, we still have a hard time forgiving ourselves. We still think about the past and it bothers us greatly. We continue to blame ourselves for all of those mistakes and failures from years ago. The past haunts us. We continue to feel guilty. We just cannot forgive ourselves for all of those bad things we have done. We feel trapped. We keeping looking back and we remember our sins all the time. We just can't let it go.

But listen: "If the Son of God sets you free, you will be free indeed." If you know the truth of God's Word, that truth will set you free. And here is God's truth: You can forgive yourself. God himself sets you free. Enter that freedom Christ has won for you. Leave the past behind and forget about it. God has forgiven your sins; you can forgive yourself, too.

Today, Jesus declares, "Don't live in the past anymore. Move forward in faith. Look to the future in faith and stop looking back. Today is the day of your salvation. Today you are set free!" Jesus says, "Continue to abide in my Word. I will help you to be my disciple. I will empower you with my Holy Spirit. Live now in my truth."

"Always remember that the Father loves you deeply. You are a redeemed child of God. Rejoice and give thanks! Let God's truth set your heart at rest. Be filled with peace and quietness. Live now in grace and serve others in love. And I will be with you always, to the very end of the age." Amen!

A GLIMPSE OF HEAVEN: Revelation 7:9-17

A frightened young man was lying in his hospital bed. He was close to dying because of complications from leukemia. The hospital chaplain walked into his room. The young man suddenly cried out, "Hey, preacher! What's the good news?"

"What's the good news?" How would you respond to that question? For the child dying of cancer in the children's hospital, for the family standing at the grave of a loved one killed in a car accident, for the family gathered around a hospice bed to say their final goodbyes, what's the good news? What can you say when your loved one dies? Where is the good news when you deal with death and dying?

Today, we have an answer to those questions. John helps us to catch a glimpse of heaven. Our text comes from an amazing vision that God showed to John. He says, "After this, I looked and a great multitude that no one could count was standing before God and the Lamb. They were wearing white robes with palm branches in their hands and were crying out with a loud voice, 'Salvation belongs to our God and the Lamb!' And all the angels of God and the people in heaven fell on their faces before the throne of God and worshipped him. They were saying, 'Amen! Blessing and glory and honor and power and might be to our God forever and ever! Amen!'"

The Lamb of God knows all about our suffering and pain. He was rejected and condemned to death. He was crucified and killed. The Lamb of God was slain, but now he reigns upon the throne of God. He who suffered so terribly during his earthly life, now rules in heaven as our risen and glorified King.

In our glimpse of heaven today, we see those who stand around the throne of God. They are now free of all the suffering and pain they experienced during their earthly life. In the presence of the Living God, there is no more pain and suffering anymore. There are no more tears and grief. No more crying and heartache. No more weeping at the graveside of a loved one. All of that has passed away and a new reality has come.

This is a new life where we will experience continual peace, joy, and blessing. This is the promise of the resurrection and eternal life after death. This is the good news we all need to hear. We can say to those who are suffering that there is something beyond their pain. There is something beyond the death of our loved ones and friends. There is something wonderful that awaits us when we depart this earthly life.

There is good news for those who grieve. "Salvation belongs to our God and to the Lamb." God wipes every tear from our eyes. Salvation belongs to God and he now bestows this gift upon his suffering people. He comforts those who mourn with the good news of the resurrection and the life of the world to come.

There is no doubt that death is our enemy. It is something we wish had never come into this world. Death brings incredible sadness and grief into our life. The pain we feel is very real. The death of our loved ones can hurt us deeply. However, there is hope. There is good news.

That is what John is trying to describe for us today. But no one, not even John, can fully describe how wonderful heaven will be. It is a reality beyond our earthly comprehension. It is beyond our ability to describe. Language fails us here. All of our best words come up short. John can only use the language and imagery of the Old Testament to describe what awaits us.

John uses pictures and images from the life of ancient Israel to describe heaven. Thus, we have tribes of people, white robes, palm branches, shepherds, and springs of flowing water in the scorching desert heat. John says, "The saints stand before the throne of God and they serve him day and night. God now shelters them with his presence. They shall not hunger or thirst anymore. The sun will not strike them or any scorching heat. For the Lamb in their midst will be their shepherd, and he will guide them to springs of living water, and God will wipe away every tear."

Our glimpse of heaven today shows us the reality of what we will experience one day. To be in heaven is to be in the very presence of the Lord Christ. In heaven, we stand in the very presence of our risen and glorified King. Jesus told his disciples, "Do not let your hearts be troubled. In my Father's house are many rooms. I am going there to prepare a place for you, so that you may be where I am."

Did you hear that? "That you may be where I am." That is precisely what John sees in his vision of heaven. He sees the Lamb of God standing in the midst of a great crowd of people from every nation around the world. They are ever so happy because they are now with God and with the Lamb forever.

Today, we remember all the saints. We remember all those who have gone before us. We remember our loved ones and friends. We remember the members of our congregation who are no longer with us. We recall all those we have known, the people we grew up with, the friendships we have shared. We miss them all terribly.

But at the same time, we know where they are. They are now experiencing the unending joy and happiness of heaven. They are in the presence of the Lamb. They are wearing their white robes and are waving palm branches in their hands. The victory is theirs. They have reached the goal. They have crossed the finish line and now stand in the winner's circle.

The key to this victory is the cross and resurrection of our Lord Jesus. He is that Lamb of God who shed his blood for us. The saints are able to stand before God because their robes have been washed white through the blood of the Lamb. We are able to stand before God only because Jesus has paid the price for our sins. He suffered and died for you. Through his holy and precious blood, your sins are forgiven. You now stand before God as clean, holy, perfect and righteous. You are a saint, one made holy by the blood of Christ.

We know that sin separates us from God. Sin creates a huge chasm between God and his people. It makes it impossible for us to enter heaven. It brings suffering and death and pain and sadness and grief into this world. "The wages of sin is death."

But now, our sin problem has been dealt with. The blood of Jesus shed on the cross atones for the sins of the whole world. He is that Lamb of God who takes away the sins of the whole world. That is why the saints gather around the throne of God. They shout for joy,

"Salvation belongs to our God and to the Lamb!"

Through faith in Christ as our Savior, we are able to catch a glimpse of heaven today. We can see a picture of what awaits all who trust in Christ. This is our confidence and hope. This is our future. Listen: We all know what this earthly life holds for us. We know that we all have to deal with trouble, heartache and grief. We will experience the loss of our loved ones. We will even experience death ourselves. Our earthly life will end. We too will one-day face dying.

However, Jesus says, "Do not let your heart be troubled. Remember that I go and prepare a place for you. I do everything necessary so that you also may be where I am in the unending glory and joy of heaven."

That is the good news today. We have a Savior who loves us and who holds our life in his hands. We catch this glimpse of heaven today, by faith, and it really strengthens us spiritually. It reminds us that we are not alone. There is always hope, even in the midst of tears and sadness.

The Lord deeply loves you. He is that Good Shepherd who guides you to the springs of living water. He wipes every tear from your eyes, and he says, "Take heart! I have overcome the world. I died for you, but behold, I am alive forevermore. Because I live, you too shall live. Be at peace. Do not let your heart be troubled."

Our Good Shepherd says, "My sheep hear my voice, and I know them, and they follow me. I give them eternal life, and they will never perish. No one can snatch them out of my hand." Amen!

RAISING CAIN: Genesis 4:1-15

Do you remember the old TV show, "The Incredible Hulk?" The main character was a scientist named Dr. David Banner. He was basically a very friendly guy. But whenever he got angry, his eyes would turn green, and he would be transformed into this big, hulking monster. Then, he would fly off into a rage. Dr. Banner did not like what anger did to him. In fact, the whole show is built around his desire to find a cure so that this will not happen to him anymore. The message here is that if you do not learn to deal with your temper, it can turn you into a monster. Anger can change you into someone you don't want to be.

This is what happened to Cain. Cain was a very angry person. He had a bad temper. In addition, it appears that he never tried to control his anger. In the end, it turned him into a violent person who committed murder. He even killed his own brother. In Genesis, we hear that Adam and Eve had two sons: Cain and Abel. Abel was a shepherd who kept flocks and Cain worked the soil as a farmer. At this point, no one has anything to complain about.

God had blessed both Cain and Abel. They both had the ability to work. They both had their health and strength. Everything seems fine. But then, there is the incident with the sacrifices. Both Cain and Abel came to worship at the same time. They both offered their gifts and offerings to the Lord. Abel's sacrifice was accepted, but Cain's was rejected. And this made Cain very angry.

I don't think that it's the nature of the sacrifice that was at issue here. It is the attitude of the worshipper that mattered. In the Old Testament, both animal and grain sacrifices were used all the time. And from what Jesus says about the widow who gave just a few pennies to the temple treasury, we know that God looks at our heart when we give our offerings. That is what makes a gift acceptable to God. It's not the amount that counts, but our attitude. And so, Cain gave his offering with the wrong attitude.

We see that also in the story of the Pharisee and the tax collector. They both went up to the temple to worship and pray. And as they stand there side-by-side, we see two different attitudes revealed. The Pharisee was smug and self-righteous. The tax collector was humble and contrite. He was the one who confessed his sinfulness to God. That was the attitude that made all the difference because God looks at our heart when we worship. He looks for honesty and truth.

Now, I have to be honest and truthful, and confess that if God were to look at my heart today, he would see a lot of unpleasant, nasty things. I am no better than Cain or the Pharisee in the temple, or anyone else in this world. I am a sinner. I also have a lot of anger and self-righteousness to deal with. And that is true for everyone today.

We certainly live in a very angry society today. Everyone is mad about something. People are furious and fed up. We are angry at so many things. We are angry with the government. We are mad about the way our boss treats us at work. We do not like our teachers at school. We get mad about the slow service we experience in restaurants and stores. We get furious at the way some people drive. We are treated badly and that makes us upset.

We are like the Incredible Hulk. Any little thing can set us off. We lose our temper. We fly off the handle. That is when we do things we later regret. We become like Cain. We give in to that sinful anger lurking in our hearts. Sin is crouching at our door. Just look again, at how Cain and Abel both offered their sacrifices. When God accepts Abel's sacrifice, Cain is furious.

But do you notice what God says to Cain? He says, "Why are you so angry all the time? If you change your attitude, won't things be better? When you lose your temper like this, sin is crouching at the door."

Here is a warning from God. "When you lose your temper, you are headed for trouble. Nothing good ever comes from it. Look out! Sin is crouching at the door." However, Cain doesn't listen to God's warning. He acts upon his anger and murders his brother. "Cain rose up against his brother and killed him." And notice how Cain felt no regret or remorse afterwards. He felt no guilt at all.

Yet again, God approaches Cain. "Where is Abel, your brother?" And Cain just shrugs his shoulders and says, "Who knows about that guy. What? Am I my brother's keeper?" That is when God speaks in judgment. God declares that Cain will be banished forever for his crime. He has to give up his occupation as a farmer and become a nomad for the rest of his life. Cain will be a fugitive, a wanderer upon the earth. Therefore, he cries out, "My punishment is more than I can bear!"

God now does a surprising thing. He has mercy. He shows grace to Cain. The Lord puts a mark on Cain so that he might be safe after he is banished. God punishes Cain, and yet shows mercy at the same time.

This reminds me of the crucifixion of our Lord Jesus Christ. When the Son of God hangs upon the cross, we see both punishment and mercy. Our Lord became our substitute when he carried our sins. He is punished so that we might receive mercy. He suffered that punishment we could never bear. Jesus suffered hell and eternal damnation.

Through that sacrificial death of Christ, we receive the mark of Cain, the sign of the holy cross. We were marked with the sign of that cross in Holy Baptism. That is a permanent mark to show that Christ the crucified has redeemed us. We have received mercy. Our sins are forgiven.

The bottom line is that we are a lot like Cain. There is a lot of anger in our hearts. Sin is crouching at our door. We also have a bad temper that gets the best of us. And if God were to punish us for every time we let anger lead us into sin, we would also cry out, "My punishment is more than I can bear!" Just like the tax collector in the temple, we have to cry out, "God, be merciful to me, a sinner!"

And the surprising thing is that God does show mercy to sinners like you and me. On the cross, the Lord Jesus cried out, "Father, forgive them for they know not what they do. Father, forgive all their anger and hatred; forgive all the hurt and pain they have caused. Father, forgive them, for the punishment is more than they can bear. I will carry their burden and give myself for them!" That is the word Jesus speaks, a word of pardon and peace. Such forgiveness cleanses our hearts and creates a right spirit within us. It creates a spirit of mercy and compassion for others.

There's no doubt we live in an angry world. Every day we encounter angry people. Every day we face situations that can provoke us and cause us to lose our tempers. So, what should we do? On a practical level, we need to learn self-control and self-discipline. We need to control our temper and not let the little things upset us so much. We cannot be like the Incredible Hulk who gets mad all the time.

On a deeper level, we need to practice confession and absolution in our personal relationships. If we sin against someone by doing something hurtful, we need to confess to them that what we did was wrong and ask for forgiveness. And the reverse is also true. If someone sins against us, we should be willing to forgive them if they repent.

The story is told of when Leonardo da Vinci was working on his famous painting of the Last Supper. He became very angry with one of his assistants who spilled some paint onto the floor. Losing his temper, Leonardo lashed out at his assistant with angry and bitter words. Returning to the painting, Leonardo attempted to finish the detail on the face of Jesus. However, he was so upset he could not compose himself for the delicate work. He stood there for a long while just gazing into the face of Christ. Finally, Leonardo put down his brush and sought out the man he had yelled at. He confessed what he did was wrong and he asked for forgiveness. The man accepted his apology and Leonardo was able to return to his work and finish painting the face of Jesus.

So, too, when we stand at the foot of the cross, we gaze up into the face of the suffering Savior. That is when we remember that we have been marked with the sign of the holy cross. We have been baptized. We need to live each day in the mercy Jesus wins for us through his passion. We need to live in mercy and not anger. We need to let go of our anger and learn to follow the way of Christ, not the way of Cain.

The devil may be raising Cain in your life, but God is able to help you deal with it. You can let go of your anger. You can control your temper. And today God says, "Go now, in peace. Your sins are forgiven. Go and live in love. Go and show mercy to all people. Go and forgive others and follow the way of my Son, Jesus Christ." Amen!

BE STRONG IN THE LORD: Ephesians 6:10-20

Today, St. Paul speaks of a battle, a spiritual battle. In this battle, we need to be strong. We need to show valor and courage. We need to stand firm when the test comes. The battle you face is not easy. Your faith will be tested. Paul says, "We struggle not against flesh and blood, but against the devil and the spiritual forces of evil." Our battle is against the very powers of darkness.

Today, God is calling you to victory. The Lord is calling you to a place that requires faith and hope. God is calling for you not to rely upon yourself, but to rely upon the Lord Jesus. Paul says, "Be strong in the Lord and in the strength of his might." All too often, we forget about these words.

Instead of relying on God's power, we try to rely on our own strength. We think we have the power to control all things. We have all the answers. We know what is best. That is why when a crisis comes into our life, we all too often ignore God and take matters into our own hands. We rely on our own power and strength. We try to fix everything ourselves.

The problem here is that some things are beyond our control. Some things we are powerless to change. Some things we cannot fix. And if we don't admit we need God's help to see us through, we are going to lose the battle. If you don't rely on God, you are going to be defeated.

That is exactly why we often feel like our life is a shambles and a wreck. We forget about God. We try to do everything by ourselves. We totally ignore God's power and help. We live our life without God. This leads to a lot of unhappiness and frustration. This fills our life with worry and stress. Some people do nothing but worry all the time. Anxiety just eats them up, resulting in ulcers, insomnia, gray hairs and a host of other health problems.

According to a recent survey: 40% of all the things we worry about will never happen; 30% of our worries involve past actions we cannot change; 20% of our worries are health-related (and our health actually gets worse the more we worry); 10% of our worries can be described as legitimate causes for concern. The bottom line is that worry and stress can have a negative effect, not only on our physical health, but also on our spiritual health. It can make us spiritually sick. We become so spiritually weak our faith collapses.

However, that is why Paul says, "Put on the whole armor of God, so that you may be able to stand against the schemes of the devil. We do not wrestle against flesh and blood, but against the spiritual forces of evil. Take up the whole armor of God and stand firm in the faith." Remember, your battle is a spiritual one. The devil tries to attack your faith. He is very subtle and deceptive. He tries to undermine your faith in any way that he can. This warfare we face is supernatural. It is invisible to the eye; yet, it is very real. And in this battle, you need to be strong in the Lord Jesus. Our victory can be found only in him.

Christ is our King. He is the One who defeats the devil. He conquers all the spiritual forces of evil. And as long as we are in Christ, we are safe in the strength of his might. Our King does what we could never do. He defeats the devil and breaks the power of darkness. He sets us free from sin and guilt. Christ bestows life and salvation. Through faith in him, you have this wondrous victory. You are set free from the past, set free from fear, set free from grief and sadness.

Listen: You may not be able to go back and change the past, but Jesus says, "Your sins are forgiven. All the mistakes of the past you so deeply regret are gone forever. Let them go! They are gone, washed away forever by my blood." You may not be able to control everything that happens in your life, but Jesus says, "I am in control of all things. I will watch over you and guide you through the days ahead. Do not live in fear, but rely upon my power and not your own." You may be having a hard time dealing with the death of a loved one, but Christ has risen from the dead. Jesus says, "There is life after death. There is hope! You will see your loved ones again in heaven. They are not lost, but they are with the Father in the glory of heaven. The Holy Spirit will now help you to cope with your grief and sorrow."

Christ is our King and Champion. He is the One who gives us everything we need so that we can stand firm in the faith. He provides us with the armor of God. He gives us protection and strength. He gives us everything necessary to make it safely through the battles we have to face. The problem is that we do not utilize these powerful resources. We forget all about the armor of God. In fact, most of us walk out of the front door every morning stark naked. Spiritually naked, that is. We expose ourselves to all kinds of spiritual attacks. We leave ourselves wide open to all kinds of temptations. We become an easy target for the devil. We are an open target spiritually.

Therefore, "Put on the whole armor of God, so that you may be able to stand against the schemes of the devil. Fasten on the strong belt of God's truth. Put on the solid breastplate of Christ's righteousness. Put on the shoes of the gospel and walk in the way of peace. Take up that shield of faith. Put on the helmet of salvation and let God's gift of eternal life put your mind at ease. Then, take up the sword of the Holy Spirit, which is the Word of God."

Paul, in effect, is saying, "Let the power of the Holy Scriptures really touch your heart and soul. Because this is how you become spiritually stronger, by putting on this defensive armor God gives you – the Word and faith in Christ." Then, Paul says, "Be sure and cover all of this armor with prayer. Pray in the power of the Holy Spirit. Pray that the Lord would help you and make you stronger. Pray that the risen Christ would protect you from evil and keep you safe." "Deliver us from evil and lead us not into temptation."

God leads you to that final victory. The Father wants you to experience his power. He wants you to stand firm and fight the good fight of faith. Never forget that Christ is your strength, he is your might. He is the foundation upon which you stand. Therefore, "Be strong in the Lord and in the strength of his might." Be strong in the Lord Jesus, and you will surely be victorious. Put on that armor of God and stand firm in the faith. The Lord is with you! Amen!

DON'T MISS THE POINT: Mark 11:1-10

The story is told of a man who took his new hunting dog on a trial run. The man went out to hunt ducks. After a while, he managed to shoot one and it fell into a lake. The dog walked on the water, picked up the duck and brought it to the hunter. The man was stunned. He shot another duck and again it fell into the lake. Once again, the dog walked on the water and brought the duck back to the hunter. He was amazed.

The next day, the hunter asked his neighbor to go hunting with him so he could show off his new dog. Just like the previous day, he shot a duck and it fell into the lake. The dog walked on the water and got it. His neighbor did not say a word. Several more ducks were shot and each time the dog walked on the water to get them. Each time, his neighbor said nothing. Finally, the hunter said, "Don't you notice anything special, anything different about my new dog?" "Yes," replied the neighbor." "Come to think of it, I do. Your dog doesn't know how to swim!"

This man completely missed the point. He couldn't see the wonder of a dog that walked on water. Sometimes we also miss the point of the coming of our Messiah King. We forget why our Savior comes to us. That is what happened to the crowds on Palm Sunday. They saw Jesus riding into Jerusalem on the back of a donkey and they waved their palm branches and shouted, "Hosanna! Blessed is he who comes in the name of the Lord! Blessed is the coming kingdom of our father David! Hosanna in the highest!"

The people greeted Jesus with cheers as he rode into Jerusalem. But did they really understand what was happening? Did they realize what kind of King Jesus truly was? Did they know why Christ came into this world? It looks like they didn't. Most of the people back then were looking for a Messiah who would free them from the Romans and their oppression.

They were looking for a king who would save them on an earthly level, a political Messiah. They thought back to the great victories that King David had won over the Philistines, the Moabites and the Ammonites. Most of the people that day were looking for someone to defeat all of their earthly enemies and to restore the theocracy to Israel. And here comes Jesus, the greater son of David, the one born in Bethlehem, the town of David, the one anointed by the Holy Spirit. And the people thought to themselves, "Surely this is our Messiah King who will now restore the kingdom to Israel. He will set us free from our enemies just like David did." Therefore, they celebrated and waved their palm branches and shouted, "Hosanna!"

However, we know this celebration would be short-lived. Just a few days later, another crowd would turn against Jesus. They would reject him. They would cry out, "Away with him! Crucify him! Crucify him!" So, what happened? Why did the people turn on Christ?

Mark tells us that after his Palm Sunday entrance, Jesus went to the temple and he chased out all the moneychangers in the temple courts and those selling merchandise in God's house. Then, for several days, the Lord Jesus would come to the temple and teach the crowds who gathered around him. He would confront the Pharisees and Sadducees. He would tell parables and quote Scripture repeatedly.

For three days, our Lord would explain who he was, and why he came, and what would happen to him. For example, after clearing the temple, Jesus said, "Is it not written in the Scriptures, 'My house will be called a house of prayer for all people?' But you have made it a den of robbers." Jesus told the Pharisees about a Son who is thrown out of the vineyard and killed. He then said, "The stone the builders rejected has become the capstone; the Lord has done this and it is marvelous in our eyes."

Then Jesus told the people how he came not to establish an earthly government or to restore the theocracy to Israel. His kingdom is not of this world. It is a spiritual kingdom, which operates by grace and forgiveness. While we live under earthly governments, pay our taxes, and fulfill our civic duties, we have a higher allegiance to God and his spiritual kingdom. Christ said, "Give to Caesar what is Caesar's, but give to God what is God."

Then, while discussing the resurrection of the dead, Jesus told the Sadducees, "You are in error because you don't know the Scriptures or the power of God. God is not the God of the dead, but the God of the living." Someone then asks the Lord, "What is the greatest commandment in the Bible?" He answers, "The greatest is this, 'Hear, O Israel, the Lord our God is one. Love the Lord your God with all your heart, your entire mind and all your strength.' The second is this: 'Love your neighbor as yourself.' There is no commandment greater than these."

Mark says that after this no one dared to ask him any more questions. Clearly, this King is someone special. He comes to do something wonderful, unique and unprecedented. This is King like no other. He cleanses God's house and restores God's people. He is that Stone rejected by the builders. But, in the end, he will become the capstone of our life. This King comes to fulfill God's law of love. He would totally love God and his neighbor. In fact, our Messiah loves us so much that he gave himself for us. He would be rejected and scorned by all. David's son would be crucified.

The crowds would mock and taunt the Christ. "If you are the King of Israel, save yourself! Come down from the cross, if you are the Son of God! Save yourself and we will believe in you." However, the Christ does not save himself. He gives up everything he has. That is the kind of King we have, a King who is thrown out of the vineyard, a King who is rejected, a King who dies on a cross. But through this death, the Scriptures are fulfilled and the power of God is revealed. God is not the God of the dead, but the God of the living. Jesus dies, but then rises from the dead. The Lord has done this and it is marvelous in our eyes! Now, God's kingdom is established. Grace is bestowed. Sins are forgiven. Death is defeated. Life is freely given. That is the real meaning of why the Son of God comes into this world.

Do not miss the point: Your King comes into your life through the power of his cross and resurrection. He comes to you in mercy and grace. Never forget that your King loves you! That is why he does all these things for you. That's why he humbles himself and suffers such rejection. And Jesus says today, "Don't miss the point of why I came. Don't forget how I suffered and died on the cross for you. Don't forget the power of my love, that power which is at work in your heart, even now." That's the real meaning of everything. Our King is the Son of God. He is the true Messiah. He is the Son of David who gave up everything so that we might receive all things.

Don't miss the point: Worship your King and joyfully hear his teaching. Devote your life to Christ and follow him each day. Live in love for God, and love your neighbor as yourself. To follow Christ means that we follow his example of mercy, love and forgiveness. We seek to love others in the very same way that Christ loved us. We share the gift we have received. We serve others and help them in their time of need. We put our faith in the Son of David. He is the capstone of our life.

Therefore, today we sing for joy, "Hosanna! Blessed is he who comes in the name of the Lord! Blessed is the coming kingdom of our father David! Hosanna in the highest!" Amen!

DEPEND ON GOD: Luke 12:22-34

A young woman brought her fiancée home to meet her parents. After dinner, her father asked the young man into his study for a chat. "So, what are your plans for the future?" the father asked. "I'm a theology student," the young man replied. "Admirable!" the father said. "But what will you do to provide for my daughter?" "I will study the Scriptures and God will provide." "But what will you do for a job?" "I don't know yet. God will provide." A bit frustrated, the father asked again, "But how will you take care of my daughter, if you don't have a job?" "God will provide." The two men left the study and the mother asked her husband, "How did it go?" The father scratched his head and said, "Well, he has no money or job. That is not so good. But even worse, he thinks I'm God!"

As Christians, we confess that we depend on God because he will provide for us. We know that ultimately God is in control of all things. However, we're not like the young man in our story. We don't just close our eyes to reality, and say, "Oh well, I'll just sit here and God will take care of me."

We realize that the Lord calls for us to put our faith into practice. We need to get to work and do our part to provide for ourselves. We work for our daily bread. God gives us the ability to work and earn a living. On the other hand, we can go too far in that direction, and end up saying, "It all depends on me! I have to do it all. If I'm ever going to be happy, I have to work as much as I can and make as much money as possible."

What we need here is a careful balance between faith and action. We trust that God will provide and that God is in control, but we also realize that we have a responsibility to put our faith into practice. It's a matter of having the right perspective and balance. Our reading from Luke 12 can help us here.

Listen again to what Jesus says, "Therefore I tell you, do not be anxious about your life. Do not worry about what you will eat, or what you will wear. Life is more than food, and the body is more than clothing. But consider the birds: They neither sow nor reap, they have neither storehouses nor barns, and yet God feeds them. And how much more valuable you are than birds! Who of you by worrying can add a single hour to his life? Since you cannot do this little thing, why do you worry about the rest?"

Notice, first of all, how the Lord says, "Do not worry so much! Your heavenly Father is in control. He takes care of all of his creation, even the birds. Don't you think he's going to take care of you?" Jesus then says, "Therefore, do not worry about what you will eat or drink. The unbelieving world runs after all such things, and your Father knows that you need them. But seek first God's kingdom, and these things will be given to you as well."

Here, we declare that we totally depend on God for everything. We confess our faith in God's providence and care. We trust in him completely, no matter what our situation may be. This means we need to set aside our worries and fears, and let go of our anxieties. It means we live by faith, trusting that God knows what is best for us and God is in control of our life.

However, that's not so easy to do, is it? It's not so easy to really trust in God and his specific plan for our life. That is why we work ourselves to the point of exhaustion, just to make sure we will one day be safe and secure. We do everything possible, so that we can finally have financial security one day. We continue to think, "I have to do it all. It all depends on me!" Somehow we never reach the point of being content and feeling secure with what we have. Despite all of our hours of work, enough is never enough. We always need just a little more. "Just a little more money, and then, I can finally be happy and content."

Of course, I am not advocating that we all quit our jobs, sit around and simply wait for the Lord to provide for all of our needs. I am not saying that we shouldn't work hard to provide for our families. But I am saying that we should allow God to play a bigger role in our life. I am advocating that we put God first in our life, and realize that ultimately, God is in control of all that happens in our life. If we can understand that, then we will have less worry and stress. We will learn to be content and finally feel secure in God's providence and care.

When we set our hearts on the things of this earth, we will surely come up short and be disappointed. If we trust only in what this world has to offer, we will always be restless and insecure. However, when we set our hearts on the things of God, we discover what is truly important. We find true and lasting treasure, the riches of God's grace and forgiveness. These true riches can set our troubled hearts at rest. Remember, the Lord Jesus says, "For where your treasure is, there your heart will be also."

So, how should we declare our dependence on God? What do we need to do? First, we need to set our priorities straight. We need to admit that our priorities in life are often inconsistent with God's will for our life.

Those two words, "I want," have become the most common phrase in our American culture today. Our daily life and thinking are totally governed by pursuing, "What I want." As a result, we constantly pursue those things we think will make us happy. We crave and desire so many different things. And we forget all about God, and what he wants us to do. Plain and simple, we should think about what God wants. We should put God first and pursue his will for our life. Then, we can stop going selfishly after our whims and desires. We can return to the Lord and learn to follow his ways.

Secondly, we need to give up our fears about our financial security and well-being. One of the most common phrases in the entire Bible is, "Fear not." Even today, we hear Jesus say, "Fear not, little flock, for it is the Father's good pleasure to give you the kingdom." God gives the kingdom as a free gift. The Father does everything necessary, so that we might have a new and better life. He does that work of salvation. We simply receive this gift, by faith. That is why we trust in Christ and depend on him for everything.

And if we can learn to trust in the Lord in such a simple way, we will find a reduction in our fear and anxiety levels. We will have less worry. We can start to have confidence and hope. A deep connection with God leads to a feeling of true and satisfying peace. We can find serenity and quietness for our troubled hearts.

There is no doubt that we all deal with worry about the future and our financial security. We are all anxious about how we will provide for our family and ourselves. This is something we all struggle with. We all worry, and we worry all the time. However, if you can learn to trust in the Lord, you discover something amazing. You can always depend upon God. He will always take care of you. He will watch over you every day.

That is precisely why Jesus says, "Do not worry so much about your life. Put aside your fears and worries about tomorrow. Trust in my heavenly Father. He knows what you need and he will provide for you." Jesus says, "Make God your top priority. Strive for his kingdom every day. Live by faith, knowing the Father is watching out for you."

That is the message today: Seek first God's kingdom and put God first in your life. If you can do that, then you will find all you need. Then, you can enjoy your life, knowing that everything is going to be okay. The Father is going to take care of you. You can depend on that. You can always depend on God! Amen!

DO NOT BE AFRAID: Matthew 10:24-33

During World War II, the Nazis persecuted churches in Germany that remained faithful to the Word of God. The Lutheran pastor, Martin Niemoeller, was on Adolf Hitler's list of people to arrest. To keep him quiet, he was put in prison. A few months later, Pastor Niemoeller was summoned before a special court, and he suddenly was filled with fear. He had no idea what to expect. Dread and apprehension gripped his heart. As he was being taken along the narrow corridor leading to the courtroom, he heard a low voice speaking from one of the cells. The voice whispered, "The name of the Lord is a strong tower; the righteous run to it and are safe."

Pastor Niemoeller later said he never knew who whispered those words, but that Bible verse had an instant impact on him. His fear vanished and his confidence in God was renewed. Trusting in God banishes fear. That is what Jesus is telling his disciples in today's reading. Today, our Lord is giving his disciples instructions prior to their first mission trip. He tells them frankly about all the dangers and hardships they would endure as they announce that the kingdom of God is near, heal the sick and share the Gospel. And just as Jesus faced opposition and persecution, so it will be for his disciples. "A student is not above his teacher, nor a servant above his master," Jesus says. "People will betray you and hand you over to the authorities. Everyone will hate you because you are my disciples."

Now, imagine that the Lord Jesus were here this morning. He now sends you out on a special mission with these same warnings. What thoughts would be racing through your mind? Perhaps something like, "No way! It is all I can do to get to church on Sundays. And I'm supposed to be shouting the Word of God from the rooftops? No way! There are other people more suited to this kind of thing. I will give this one a pass. Let someone else do it!"

No doubt, Jesus is sending his disciples out like sheep in the midst of wolves. So, what does the Lord do? Sell them life insurance? Give them a quick course in martial arts and self-defense? No, instead Jesus urges them to trust God. Confidently go ahead and speak the truth. Shout it out! Stand fast in your faith and do the work of the Lord. Share the good news and tell all people about the kingdom of God.

"Do not be afraid," Jesus says, "Are not two sparrows sold for a penny? Yet not one of them falls to the ground apart from the will of your Father. And even the very hairs of your head are all numbered. So, do not be afraid; you are worth more than many sparrows."

Sparrows are very common birds. We may think they are small and insignificant creatures, yet, they matter to God. Sparrows are special to our heavenly Father.

What about your hair? When you were having your last haircut, did the barber say to you, "Did you know that hair number 574 has a split end?" But Jesus says that every hair on your head is numbered. And he says that God is vitally interested in hair number 574, even though you might consider it too trivial to worry about. You see, our Lord wants to teach us that it doesn't matter what may be happening in our life, God has an intimate knowledge of every detail.

You may think that no one understands what you are going through in your life right now. It may be you are suffering in silence. Others don't appreciate the depth of your anguish and pain. However, God knows. God knows and sees everything. And he knows in perfect detail everything going on in your life right now.

Isn't that amazing? Our God knows everything that we go through. Nothing that happens to us escapes him. When we feel lonely and abandoned, when it seems that our prayers are unanswered, when everything seems totally hopeless - God knows and he cares. Jesus says, "So, do not be afraid; you are worth much more than many sparrows. Do not be afraid!" "Do not be afraid," Jesus says. We certainly live in a fearful world. We look around and we see many things that fill us with fear. It is getting scary out there. This is a crazy world. We do not know what's going to happen next. And that can fill us with dread and apprehension. The future is frightening.

What it all boils down to is this: The perfect antidote for fear is trust in the Lord. Faith is what we all need. That is the experience that Pastor Niemoeller had as he was being taken down the corridor of a Nazi prison to an indefinite future. An unknown voice whispered, "The name of the Lord is a strong tower; the righteous run to it and are safe." That Bible verse reminded Pastor Niemoeller that God knew his situation. God would give him the strength to face whatever lay ahead. His fear vanished. Confidence and trust were restored. His faith was strengthened.

The Bible is full of powerful messages about trusting God in times of trouble. For example, in the opening of Psalm 27, we hear, "The Lord is my light and my salvation: Whom shall I fear? The Lord is the stronghold of my life: Of whom shall I be afraid? For in the day of trouble, he will keep me safe in his dwelling, he will hide me in the shelter of his tabernacle and set me high upon a rock. Hear my voice when I call, O Lord, be merciful to me and answer me."

We hear such verses from the Psalms and are strengthened. We can even say that this was the experience of Jesus as he faced the horror of the cross. He went to the Garden of Gethsemane and prayed just such Psalm verses. At Gethsemane, we see how the Teacher goes before his students. The Lord goes before his servants. He suffers for our salvation and he calls for us to follow him into his passion. Jesus had feelings and emotions just like any other human. Even though he was the Son of God, he was also true man, flesh and blood just like us. And the prospect of suffering and dying for the sins of the whole world filled our Lord with dread and apprehension. He even told his disciples, "My soul is overwhelmed with sorrow, even to the point of death."

We should never think that suffering hell and damnation on behalf of the sins of all humanity was a light and easy thing for Christ to do. In the Garden of Gethsemane, we see the honest struggle he endured for us. And our Lord emerged from this struggle with renewed confidence and strength. At the end, he said, "Not my will be done, O Father, but yours."

Jesus was obedient to the Father. He left the Garden of Gethsemane and faced the cross with determination and strength. Our Lord willingly suffered the passion. He went the way of suffering, rejection and betrayal. Our Teacher dies and suffers our punishment. He gives himself for us. Here we see the love of God revealed so clearly. He died so that we might live. He suffered so that we might have that promise of the forgiveness of sins. Our Teacher goes before us into death, burial and resurrection. Then, after his resurrection on Easter morning, Jesus appeared to his disciples for a period of 40 days. During that time, he was teaching them and preparing them for the world mission they would soon embark on.

We know that later, after the ascension of Christ into heaven, the disciples faced all kinds of persecution. They were rejected and betrayed. They would be persecuted even to the point of losing their lives. The early followers of Jesus faced hatred and opposition. Their life would constantly be in danger. However, these words of Christ we hear today had a powerful effect on these early Christians as they suffered for their faith. It was a great comfort to know that they were not suffering alone. Their heavenly Father knew exactly what they were going through and what was happening to them.

If God knows all about one hair that falls from our head, or a small ordinary bird, then how much more does he know about us? The Father knows what his people have to face. He sees our situation and difficulties, and he cares. There's no doubt that sometimes we are afraid. We are afraid of so many things. We are afraid of what others will think of us if we speak up for Christ and confess our faith. We are afraid of what the future may bring to us. We are afraid of getting older. We are afraid of our health failing. We are afraid of death and dying.

Whatever trouble or crisis is affecting your life today, God knows your troubles, and he knows better than you would ever think. Even if no one else cares about you or understands your pain, be assured your heavenly Father knows exactly what is happening in your life, and he cares.

God cares for you. He is on your side; your life is in his hands. "The name of the Lord is a strong tower; the righteous run to it and are safe." The next time fear takes a grip on your life, take a moment to recall some of the great promises of God. Remember what Christ suffered for you. Read the Psalms and pray them aloud. Make the words of the Psalms your very own by using them in your prayers.

Remind yourself that God cares about you. You are a dear child of his and you are deeply loved. You are special in God's eyes. And always remember that you are a disciple of the Lord Jesus. You are a student of the Teacher, a servant of the Lord. And your Teacher says, "Be prepared and ready. If you follow me, you may suffer, too. If they persecuted me, they may persecute you as well. A student is not above his teacher, nor a servant above his master. It is enough for the student to be like his teacher, and the servant like his master."

Do not be afraid! But go and proclaim the good news. Stand fast in the faith, and do the work of God's kingdom. Share your faith and confess that Christ is your Lord and Savior. Continue to trust and believe. And always remember, "The name of the Lord is a strong tower; the righteous run to it and are safe." Amen!

A TRICKY THING: Luke 17:11-19

Imagine these ten guys. Imagine the leprosy, the pain. All alone and isolated, separated from the rest of the community. They spot Jesus on his way to Jerusalem. The Lord comes walking right into their life. They cry out for help. "Jesus, Master, have pity on us!" "Go, show yourselves to the priests."

And with that, Jesus sends them on their journey. Ten of them, on the way. All of them healed. However, one, only one comes back, giving thanks. Jesus asks the obvious, "Were not all ten cleansed? Where are the other nine?"

We have come today before the Lord to worship him. We have come to hear his Word, to receive his gifts and to give thanks. We all are coming back in one way or another. We come to give thanks to a loving God who has graciously redeemed us with the blood of the Lamb.

Let me ask you: "Whom do you identify with in this story?" The nine who didn't come back to express thanks? Or the one who returned, praising God and giving thanks to the Lord? Note again the reaction of the one leper. Luke says, "One of them, when he saw he was healed, came back, praising God in a loud voice. He threw himself at Jesus' feet and thanked him." This man was so grateful. He couldn't thank him enough. And Jesus says, "Rise and go! Your faith has made you well."

This gratitude thing is tricky. It seems like the more blessings we receive, the less thankful we become. The more generosity we experience, the more we take it for granted. Is there someone in your life you take for granted? A husband or wife, a son or daughter, a mother or father? Do you take your good health for granted? Are you thankful for what you have today? Are you thankful for food, clothing and shelter? Are you thankful for family and friends? Or do you take all that for granted?

Very often, rather than having a heart filled with gratitude and thanks, we find ourselves complaining about our family, our health and our finances. We complain so much about our life. We grumble and murmur.

What do you think happened to the other nine? Why didn't they come back filled with gratitude? Why didn't they return to Jesus? Maybe they thought they deserved good health: they had suffered enough. Maybe they thought they just got lucky: they had hit the jackpot. Maybe they didn't have time: life is so hectic and busy.

This gratitude thing is tricky. It is easier to take things for granted than to be grateful. Some of you can remember how the Lord heard your call for help. That healthy child that was born to you. You just couldn't have been more thankful to God. But somehow, you became less thankful over time. That near brush with death that restored your appreciation for the gift of life. Somehow, that gratitude was brushed aside. Or that answer to that special prayer. God helped you in such a wonderful way. That meant so much to you back then, but now, it has faded with time.

Gratitude is a tricky thing. If you asked any of those ten men afflicted with that dreadful disease of leprosy, they would have told you about the pain and suffering they experienced. They would have told you about the separation that isolated them from family and friends. They would have talked about their loneliness, sadness and despair. They all desperately wanted a new life. That is why they cried out for help. "Jesus, Master, have pity on us!"

We often feel that way, too. You can identify with those ten lepers. You have felt the pain. You are hurt and wounded inside. You're not sure that God hears your prayers. You are not sure that God cares about you. You can't understand why bad things happen to you.

You say, "If only Jesus would walk down my road! If only the Lord would give me a new life, a new chance, a new beginning!" That is the beautiful thing about today's message. I have some good news for you! The Lord Jesus Christ has walked down your road. He says to you, "Rise and go! Your faith has made you well." That's what salvation is all about.

In Jesus Christ, God has come into your life. The Bible says, "In the fullness of time, God sent forth his Son to be born of a woman, born under law, to redeem those under the law." In Christ, God comes into our world and into our life. The Bible also says, "Cast all your cares upon him, for he cares for you." And Jesus says, "Lo, I am with you always, to the end of the age."

You see, Christ wanted to do more than just heal those ten lepers and send them on their way. He wanted to heal their relationship with God. He wanted to restore to them the joy of salvation. That is something we all need.

Back when God first created the world, he saw that it was "very good." Creation was perfect. And on the sixth day, when God created mankind, he saw that the man and woman were perfect. Adam and Eve had perfection. They were perfectly happy and healthy. They had a perfect and complete relationship with God. They had food to eat, a place to live, healthy bodies and a purpose to life. Yet, Adam and Eve took all that for granted. They were unthankful.

Before long, they focused on the forbidden. They saw what they didn't have. They desired what they didn't need. They wanted to be "like God," that is, they wanted to be greater and wiser than God. Then came the fall. Our relationship with our Creator was broken. And so began the long story of sin. It is a sad story of misery, pain and woe, a story of separation and broken relationships, a story of death.

I hope that you can see yourself in this story of what happened in the Garden of Eden. It explains why the world is the way it is today. It explains why bad things happen in our life and why sin and death exist. However, that is not the end of the story.

After the fall of Adam and Eve, God spoke to them again and he spoke a word of grace. God spoke about a Savior who would be born of the woman, someone who would crush the head of the serpent. A promised One. A healer. This Savior would live a perfect life on our behalf. He would die for us.

Jesus Christ is our healer. His love heals our broken hearts. His grace heals our sin-sickness. "By his wounds, we are healed." The cross of Jesus heals our broken life. He became our substitute. He took our place on the cross. He offered up his perfect life to atone for our guilt. Our Lord was punished for us. Truly, he is that Lamb of God who takes away the sin of the world. He shed his blood, died, and was buried. Then he rises from the dead.

And now, more than anything else, Christ wants to bestow upon you the gift of salvation. He wants to heal your disease of sin, he wants to remove the scars from your soul. He wants to take away your loneliness and pain and bring you into a new life. Our Savior heals our sin-sickness and our leprosy is gone. We are made whole. In this way, Christ restores our relationship with God. He brings us back to the Father and restores to us the joy of salvation.

And so, today we have a simple story from the life of Christ. Ten lepers, lost and lonely. Ten lepers going nowhere. However, they cross paths with the Savior. He comes walking into their life and things are never the same. Nine go on their way and do their thing.

But one came back, praising God with a loud voice. He threw himself at Jesus' feet and he thanked him. He was so grateful. He couldn't thank him enough. That's how it is when the grace of God touches your life. That's how it is when the Lord Jesus Christ touches your heart and soul. God's gift gives life – a new life in Christ!

In this new life, we have a heart filled with gratitude. In this new life, we no longer take anything for granted. We are now so thankful for our family and friends, for our health, for our possessions and wealth. We now give thanks to God for his many blessing and we now desire to serve our Lord with our whole life. We now gladly come to worship. We praise God, throw ourselves down at Jesus' feet and truly thank him. And then, we hear that Word of the Lord that says, "Rise and go! Your faith has made you well. Go now in peace!" Amen!

AN UP AND DOWN LIFE: John 16:5-33

Luke tells us in the first chapter of Acts that after Jesus rose from the dead, he spent 40 days teaching his disciples about the kingdom of God. Jesus explained to them the meaning of his cross and resurrection. "Did not the Christ have to suffer these things and then enter into his glory?" Jesus also told them, "Do not leave Jerusalem, but wait for the gift my Father promised. John baptized with water, but in a few days, you will be baptized with the Holy Spirit. You will receive power when the Spirit of God comes upon you. You will then be my witnesses in Jerusalem, in all Judea and Samaria and to the ends of the earth."

Then, Jesus led his disciples outside of the city to the Mount of Olives and while they were all watching, he ascended into heaven. He was taken up into the sky before their very eyes. They watched Jesus disappear until the clouds hid him from their sight. The disciples stood there for a long time, looking up intently up into the sky. Suddenly, two angels appeared. They said, "Why do you stand here looking up into the sky? This same Jesus, who was taken from you into heaven, will come back in the same way you have seen him go into heaven."

Today, we look at the ascension of our Lord. There are at least two ways of looking at this unique event. First of all, you can stand there with the disciples and look up into the sky. You can stand there and watch until Jesus disappears off into the clouds.

In this upward vision, there is that wonderful motion and movement toward the skies. It is up, up and away. Here is the promise of great things to come. Christ returns to that glory that has always been his as the Son of God. He returns to the heavenly Father. As Jesus tells his disciples, "I came from the Father and have come into the world. And now, I am leaving this world and going to the Father."

In the last chapters of Revelation, you catch a glimpse of the incredible glory of heaven. The new Jerusalem, the heavenly city of God, is described in fantastic imagery. The glory of the Lord God Almighty and the Lamb shines forth in brilliant splendor. God promises to make all things new.

John says, "Then I saw a new heaven and earth, for the first heaven and earth had passed away. And I saw the holy city, the new Jerusalem, coming down out of heaven from God, prepared as a bride adorned for her husband. And I heard a loud voice from the throne saying, 'Now, the dwelling place of God is with man. He will dwell with them, and they will be his people, and God himself will be with them. He will wipe every tear from their eyes, and death shall be no more, neither shall there be mourning or crying or pain anymore, for the former things have passed away.' And he who was seated on the throne said, 'Behold, I am making all things new!'"

Here, we lift up our hearts for a foretaste of the feast to come. This is a glimpse of the future that awaits us. We look and we feel a sense of promise, hope and eager expectation. We look forward to the resurrection of the dead and the life of the world to come.

Jesus told his disciples, "Do not let your hearts be troubled. Trust in God; trust also in me. In my Father's house are many rooms. I am going there to prepare a place for you. And if I go and prepare a place for you, I will come back and take you to be with me, that you also may be where I am."

Jesus reminds us that in the Father's house there is plenty of room. In addition, our Lord goes before us and he prepares a place for us. Christ has ascended into heaven to make reservations for us. Everything has been prepared and made ready so that we may dwell with God in the heavenly Jerusalem. He goes to prepare a place for us.

However, there is another dimension to consider as well. The ascension of our Lord has another angle to it, and I suspect this angle is closer to the reality we have to face each day. I suspect that there was more gloom than rejoicing on the Mount of Olives that day. I bet that after the disciples watched the Lord disappear into the clouds, they felt lost and confused. They probably felt abandoned and left behind.

For 40 days after the resurrection, the disciples enjoyed the intense fellowship of the Lord. But now he is taken away from them. The Lord sails off into the sky and disappears. Jesus is gone – what do we do now? The Lord has left us – how are we going to survive? This is how we feel sometimes, too.

It is truly an up and down life for us. Things are good for a while, but then they are bad. We sometimes say, "My life is so hard. I am really struggling here. I don't know how I'm going to cope with all the troubles and sorrows I have to face. Heaven's alright for those who are there, but what about us who are left behind?"

Okay, true enough. However, remember this: The ascension is not simply saying, "Goodbye," to a departing Jesus. It is not simply upward in its motion. There is an earthly dimension to it as well and this is where we come in. We are just like the disciples on the Mount of Olives that day.

Like the disciples, we are called to get on with the task of living out our faith each day. We are not permitted the luxury of standing there and gazing up into the sky. No, we must get on with the Lord's work. We are called to go forth, and to witness, serve, and work for God's kingdom. We are called to love and care for others, to help those in need, to show God's compassion and mercy to all people.

Remember how Jesus told his disciples before he ascended, "Do not leave Jerusalem. But wait for the gift my Father promised." Despite whatever we may think, we are not alone. The Lord Jesus has given us the Holy Spirit. He is the promised gift. The Holy Spirit is the Comforter, the Counselor, the Lord and Giver of life. The Spirit helps us make it through this difficult life.

The Spirit is the Comforter who wipes away our tears. He bestows his solace and care upon us. He helps us to cope with the sorrows and heartaches we have to face. He is with us as we grieve.

The Spirit is the Counselor who guides and directs us through this earthly life. He shows us the way to go. The Spirit instructs us through God's Word. Scripture says, "Direct me in the path of your commands, for there I find delight." "Your Word is a lamp to my feet and a light for my path." The Holy Spirit helps us to find our way in this confusing world.

The Spirit is also the Lord and Giver of life. He opens our hearts to receive God's gift of salvation in Christ. We are born again by the

Holy Spirit, who now works through the Word and Holy Baptism to give us life and salvation. Scripture says, "Flesh gives birth to flesh, but the Spirit gives birth to spirit." "God has saved us through the washing of rebirth and renewal by the Holy Spirit." "You were washed, you were sanctified, you were justified in the name of the Lord Jesus Christ and by the Spirit of our God."

That is the good news today: The Holy Spirit is at work in your heart and soul. You have received the same gift that the first disciples received. You have been washed, sanctified, and justified by the Spirit of God. The Holy Spirit is your Comforter and Counselor. Jesus tells us, "When the Spirit of truth comes, he will guide you into all the truth. He will declare to you all I have done for you. He will glorify me, for he will take what is mine and declare it to you."

Now, it is true: It is an up and down life for all of us. We all have those difficult challenges in life that we have to face. However, there is help. There is the gift the Father promised. Our Lord Jesus speaks about asking for the gift. He says, "Ask and you will receive. Ask and your joy will be complete." Jesus speaks repeatedly about the gift the Father promised; this is the gift of the Holy Spirit.

Jesus says, "Ask for the Holy Spirit and he will come into your heart. Pray, and he will help you, guide you and counsel you. He will bless you and renew your faith."

Our Lord says to each of us, "I am going to the Father to prepare a place for you. Take heart; I will not leave you all alone. I will send the Holy Spirit. He will comfort and counsel you. He will lift up your eyes to see the promise of heaven and God's new creation to come. He will empower you to be my witness, my servant and my disciple."

Jesus says, "Ask, and you receive all of this. Then, your joy will be complete. Ask for the gift of the Holy Spirit and he will bless you, both now and forevermore!" Amen!

IN THE CROSS OF CHRIST I GLORY: John 3:1-21

A visitor to Sweden tells the story of a little country church located there. It is not a particularly beautiful church. There is nothing exceptional about it, except for one thing. When you go inside the church, you notice that there is a large, life-size crucifix hanging on the wall opposite the pulpit. The figure of our Lord is life-like, even to the use of real hair beneath the crown of thorns. How did such a huge crucifix happen to be in a Swedish Lutheran church?

Well, it seems that in the early 1700's, the king of Sweden paid an unexpected visit to the church one Sunday morning. When the pastor saw the king in attendance, he was totally overwhelmed. Instead of preaching on the text for that Sunday, he gave a fawning tribute to the king. Soon afterward, the church received the crucifix from the king. With it came this command: "Hang this within the church so that whoever stands in the pulpit will always remember the words of St. Paul, 'We preach Christ crucified.'"

Today, our eyes turn to the cross of our Lord Jesus. When we look at the cross of our Lord, we see suffering, pain and death. However, if we look again with the eyes of faith, we see something more. We see the love of God at work for our salvation. Jesus says, "Just as Moses lifted up the serpent in the wilderness, so must the Son of Man be lifted up. For God so loved the world, that he gave his only Son, that whoever believes in him should not perish but have eternal life."

The cross of Jesus is a symbol of pain and suffering. That is true. However, at the same time, it is a symbol of joy and freedom. This is true because through the cross, we are set free from the bonds of sin and the chains of death. We are set free to be God's people and to live in true joy and happiness. The cross of Jesus transforms everything it touches.

Such is the incredible power of the cross of Jesus. This power flows from the love of God. "For God so loved this fallen world that he gave his one and only Son to suffer and die on the cross for our sins." God the Father loves this world, which he created. Even though we sinned and rebelled against our Creator, God still seeks our salvation. The Lord does not want us to be condemned and lost. He does not want us to perish in eternal damnation. He doesn't want us to be separated from him any longer.

The Father gives us his Son. He gives us a way back home, a way out of sin and death, a way out of eternal condemnation and hell.

Look again and see how much God loves you! Just as Moses lifted up the snake on the pole in the desert, so the Son of Man was lifted up on the cross, so that everyone who looks to him in faith might be rescued from the snakebite of sin and death. God provides a way of salvation. All we have to do is look and see.

When we look, we do see how the Son of God hangs upon that rough, wooden cross. We see the spikes driven through his hands and feet. We see the crown of thorns on his head. We see the incredible pain and suffering. We see the blood and the wounds. But look again and you will see the love of God revealed so clearly. You will see how the innocent One suffers for the guilty. You will see how the perfect One gives his life for the imperfect. You will see the Holy One of God bearing our burden and carrying our sins. Look to cross in faith and you will see Jesus.

He takes all of our sin and guilt upon himself and he carries it down into the depths of hell where it belongs. He dies for us on that cross. Then, he rises from the dead in glory and light. Jesus conquers death for our salvation. Christ now brings us into the bright sunshine of God's love. Our Lord brings us into a new life of joy and freedom. This is why we rejoice in God's gifts of grace. We praise our Lord and magnify his holy name. We sing our hymns with joy and gladness. We sing:

In the cross of Christ I glory,
  Towering over the wrecks of time.
All the light of sacred story,
  Gathers round its head sublime.
When the woes of life overtake me,
  Hopes deceive and fears annoy.
Never shall the cross forsake me;
  Lo, it glows with peace and joy.

The writer of this famous hymn was John Bowring. He wrote these words in the early 1800's after he visited Macao on the South China Coast. Macao had just been struck by a massive typhoon. In the harbor were the wrecks of all the ships sunk by the powerful storm. On a hill, overlooking the harbor was a huge cathedral originally built by the early Portuguese colonists. This cathedral had been almost completely destroyed by the typhoon. Only one wall was still standing. On top of that wall was a huge bronze cross shining brightly in the morning sunlight.

John Bowring was so impressed by the shining cross standing tall and true after the terrible storm, he wrote the words to our hymn. These words remind us that even in the midst of the worst storms we may experience, the cross of Jesus stands tall and true. His love continues to shine forth even in the midst of our darkest woes.

God shines his light upon us and we remember once again that we are safe in God's love. His love and grace will see us through. We can cope with whatever storm we are facing in our life right now. We can live in peace and joy. We can make it, if the cross goes before us. "When the woes of life overtake me, hopes deceive and fears annoy. Never shall the cross forsake me; Lo, it glows with peace and joy." Always remember: "God so loved the world that he gave his only Son." This makes all the difference in the world. This changes us forever. Consider the following story.

A young woman was riding on the subway. She was wearing a shiny gold cross on a chain. It was pretty and she considered it special. A man sitting across from her noticed her cross. He said sarcastically, "Young lady, I imagine you think Jesus died on the cross for you. If he really did, I don't think that cross was shiny and pretty like the one you are wearing. It was an ugly wooden thing. The Romans used it to execute criminals. Frankly, I don't understand why you would wear such a thing as a piece of jewelry. Would you wear a hangman's noose or an electric chair around your neck?"

The young woman was stunned by his harsh words. She thought for a moment and then said, "Yes, it's true, I believe that Jesus died for me on a cross. And I know that his cross was not as pretty as mine. But I also know what they told me in Sunday School." "And what was that?" the man asked. She answered, "In

Sunday School, my teacher told me that whatever Jesus touches, he changes. I think that is true for this cross. I know that it is true for me. I have been changed by the power of his love. That is what this cross means for me!"

Yes, that's so true. The love of God is clearly revealed through the cross of Jesus. That love is powerful and effective. It changes us forever. It transforms all who believe in the Son of God. When Jesus touches your life, you are changed.

The cross means that God loves you. He wants for you to have life, and to have it to the full. That is why the Father gave his Son to die on the cross for you. That's why he shines his light upon you. God wants for you to live each day in his sunlight. He wants for you to rejoice in the freedom he bestows. Receive his peace and blessing today. Live by the truth of God's Word and come into his light.

Jesus says, "For God did not send his Son into the world to condemn the world, but to save the world through him. Whoever lives by the truth comes into the light, so that it may be seen plainly that what he has done has been done by God."

Look again and see how much God loves you! Behold the gift of God's love in Christ. Let that love touch your life today and change your heart. In the cross of Christ, I glory! Amen!

AT THE KING'S TABLE: Luke 22:7-38

"Then came the day of Unleavened Bread, on which the Passover Lamb had to be sacrificed. Jesus sent Peter and John, saying, 'Go and make preparations for us to eat the Passover.'" We begin today with the Passover Lamb which had to be sacrificed. We begin with Jesus, and we see how he is in total control of the situation. He wants to enjoy this last meal with his disciples and he does not want to be disturbed by the police knocking on the door.

If you recall, Judas had already made a deal with the chief priests to betray Jesus over to them at the first opportunity. However, the Lord is prepared. He has made arrangements with the owner of a large house in Jerusalem. By doing this quietly ahead of time, he prevented Judas from betraying him prematurely. Christ would suffer and die, but in his own good time, not when his enemies chose. None of his disciples knew ahead of time where the Passover meal would be held. The Lord was in total control of these events as they unfold. He knows exactly what will happen soon.

When the hour came, Jesus and his apostles reclined at the table. He said to them, "I have eagerly desired to eat this Passover with you before I suffer. For I tell you, I will not eat it again until it finds fulfillment in the kingdom of God." Our Savior speaks repeatedly about the kingdom of God, the kingdom he confers upon us. In this kingdom, we eat and drink at the King's Table. The Lord is among us as one who serves.

In Luke's account of the Lord's Supper, there are several themes that are skillfully woven together. There is an emphasis on how the King celebrates his Supper with his disciples. He knows that it will be his last meal with them for now. However, he speaks of eating again with them in the future, when God's kingdom comes in its fullness.

Luke is the only Gospel that tells us about the two disciples traveling on the way to Emmaus on the afternoon of the first Easter. A stranger appeared and joined them on their journey. This stranger spoke with them at length about the events that occurred in the city of Jerusalem that weekend. He explained the meaning of Good Friday and why the Messiah had to suffer.

Towards the end of the day, the two disciples invited the stranger to eat with them. During the meal, they recognized the risen Christ as he took the bread and broke it. Their eyes were opened to see that Jesus was truly present before them. They were now at the King's Table. They discerned the real presence of Christ.

Jesus knew that he would eat and drink again with his disciples to prove that he really was alive again. He proves that the kingdom of God has arrived. This kingdom comes to us only through his cross and resurrection. And we are now privileged to eat and drink at our King's Table.

Another theme that Luke presents is the Passover meal itself. This was a time of remembrance. The people of Israel were to remember the Exodus and how God had saved his people from Egypt. God rescued his people from their slavery and bondage. Each part of the Passover meal was designed to remind the people of what had happened for their salvation. The bitter herbs were a reminder of the bitter and harsh conditions of their slavery. The unleavened bread taught them that they had to leave in haste. The Passover Lamb was sacrificed for their deliverance. The blood of the Lamb rescued them from the judgment that fell upon Egypt.

In the context of this Passover meal, Jesus now creates a new meal of remembrance. He took the bread, gave thanks and broke it. He then gave it to his disciples and said, "This is my body, given for you. Do this in remembrance of me." In the same way, after the supper, he took the cup of wine and said,

"This cup is the new covenant in my blood, which is poured out for you."

Our Lord speaks of his body given unto death. He says, "It is given for you." That is the heart of this meal: He dies for YOU on the cross. He dies for your sins. Christ also speaks of his blood, which is poured out. He sheds his blood for YOU. The blood of the Lamb rescues you from judgment. This is the new covenant which God the Father establishes through the sacrifice of his Son. This is a New Exodus, which includes all of humanity. It brings forgiveness for all sinners. It works a mighty deliverance from the bondage of death and despair. It bestows life - a new life that will never end.

Our Lord says, "Do this in remembrance of me." "Do this, as you recall and remember everything I have done for you. Remember how I suffered the passion! Never forget this great sacrifice I am making for you. Remember how much I love you!" Jesus says, "Greater love has no one than this, that he lay down his life for his friends. And you are my friends."

When we partake of the Lord's Supper, we focus upon how our Passover Lamb has been sacrificed. We remember our Exodus from the slavery of sin and guilt. We rejoice that we have been saved from eternal death and damnation. We celebrate the new covenant God bestows upon us through Christ.

But amazingly, even as Jesus institutes his Supper, a dispute arose among the disciples as to which of them is the greatest. Can you imagine that? Jesus is talking about what he is about to suffer and the disciples are arguing about who is the greatest, who is strongest, who will prevail unto the end.

The disciples are concerned with their status and place within God's kingdom. They want to be first and to be the greatest. Yet, very soon, within just a few hours, they will all fail. They will forsake Jesus and run away. The apostles will fall apart and fail. They will all scatter and flee when Jesus is arrested. Even Peter will deny knowing Jesus before a large crowd of people, not just once, but three times.

Here is a powerful reminder that the Lord's Supper is meant for sinners, for people who fail to follow Jesus. It is meant for people like you and me. Sometimes we may think, "Well, I'm not good enough to go to Communion this week."

But the truth is this: None of us are "good enough" to go to the Lord's Supper. If partaking of the Lord's Supper depended upon our level of goodness, none of us could ever go. All of us are sinners. We are no different from the disciples. We approach the

King's Table and we confess that we are unworthy of the great gifts our Lord bestows here. We confess our sinfulness and our unfaithfulness. We are failures. We are sinners. But we also confess that our Passover Lamb has been sacrificed. There is cleansing and forgiveness. There is hope and there is life. There is the body and blood of Christ, given and shed for you and me.

When the disciples argued about status and greatness within God's kingdom, Jesus said, "The kings of the Gentiles lord it over them. And those who exercise authority call themselves Benefactors. But you are not to be like that. Instead, the greatest among you should be like the youngest and the one who rules like one who serves. For who is greater, the one who is at the table or the one who serves? Is it not the one who is at the table? But I am among you as one who serves."

Note how the Lord speaks of himself as "one who serves." This shows us how the eternal Son of God humbles himself in obedience to the Father's will. The King who rules over all of creation will become our servant. He will wash our feet. The greatest will become the lowest. The Son of God will be "numbered with the transgressors." He will be crucified in the middle of two criminals. He will take the lowest place with sinners as he dies on the cross.

That is what we remember as we approach the King's Table today. Our King will wear a crown of thorns. He will become the least, the last and the littlest as he carries our sins. He will give his body into suffering and death. He will pour out his blood to atone for our guilt. He will become our substitute. This is true greatness: Service, sacrifice, humility. "I am among you as one who serves." "Greater love has no one than this, that he lay down his life for his friends. And you are my friends." This is amazing!

The King calls us his friends and he invites us to his Supper. As we gather around his Table once again, he serves us his Supper. We again hear those words, which Christ spoke on the night he was betrayed by Judas, "This is my body, given for you. This cup is the new covenant in my blood, which is poured out for you. Do this in remembrance of me."

As we hear these Words and remember our Lord's great sacrifice for us, the Holy Spirit opens our eyes. Like the disciples on the way to Emmaus, we now suddenly realize that Christ is truly present as he breaks the bread. We now discern the Lord's real presence. The risen Christ is with us in this meal. The Holy Spirit opens our hearts to see the power of God's love in Christ. Jesus says, "The Holy Spirit will teach you all things and will remind you of everything I have said to you." That is so true!

The Holy Spirit reminds us of what Christ said and did, on the night he was betrayed. He teaches us the true meaning of greatness within God's kingdom. He shows how to be humble servants, people who are willing to love and serve others. We give of ourselves to others, in the same way Christ gave himself for us.

We rejoice that we belong to Christ and our life is in his hands. You now belong to the King and are a part of his kingdom! You are privileged, indeed, to eat and drink at the King's Table. Amen!

BELIEVING THE SCRIPTURES: John 2:13-22

When Jesus came to the temple in Jerusalem, he was confronted with commercialism running riot. Instead of a quiet, reverent place where people could pray and worship, there was a noisy trading center. People were selling oxen, sheep, lambs, pigeons and doves. They were exchanging money so that the people could make their offerings in the local currency.

While all of this business activity may have been necessary for the worshippers who had travelled a long way from foreign places, there was no need to drag this dog and pony show inside the temple courts. It turned the house of God into a State Fair.

Therefore, when Jesus saw all of this he became angry. He made a whip out of cords and began to drive all of these animals out of the temple courts. He said, "Get these animals out of here! How dare you turn my Father's house into a marketplace!" He flipped over the tables of the moneychangers and poured out their coins upon the ground.

This cleansing of the temple by Jesus was a Messianic deed. It was a supreme and mighty announcement that one greater than the temple has arrived. The religious authorities of Israel immediately notice this. They confront Jesus and demand to know why he is doing this.

They say, "What miraculous sign can you show us to prove your authority to do all this?" And Jesus answers, "Destroy this temple and I will raise it again in three days." Here, our Lord gives us the sign of his resurrection. As Jesus would later say, "For as Jonah was three days and nights in the belly of the fish, so the Son of Man will be three days and nights in the heart of the earth."

This is the only sign that Jesus was willing to give. The religious leaders demand that he prove his authority to do all of these things, and Jesus says, "Destroy this temple and I will raise it again in three days." "And the temple he spoke of was his body."

That is the only sign given to us: The death and resurrection of the Messiah of Israel. This is God's universal sign given to the whole world. If you are wondering if all of this stuff about Jesus is true, if you are looking for a sign that God's Word is true, if you need some kind of proof that Jesus is the Savior – that sign has been given. Christ has risen!

The religious leaders totally misunderstood what Jesus is saying. They interpret his words in a strange way, as if he were claiming he could perform an architectural impossibility.

They say, "We have been working on this building project for forty-six years, and we still aren't finished. How can you raise it in three days?" Now, think about those words: "How can you raise it in three days?" That is a great question. That really summarizes our human unbelief when it comes to the things of God. "How can this be?" we ask. We are like little children confronted by something beyond our comprehension.

I remember, long ago I told a Bible story to a class of our nursery school. I told the story of Bartimaeus to a group of preschoolers. Jesus healed the blind beggar in Jericho. You remember that story. The Lord was passing through Jericho. A big parade formed and the people were all excited. Suddenly, this old beggar spoiled everything. He starts shouting at the top of his lungs, "Jesus, Son of David, have mercy on me!"

The Lord stops the whole parade and called the blind man to himself. He asked, "What do you want?" "I want to see," Bartimaeus simply answered. Jesus said, "Go! Your faith has healed you." And immediately, the blind man received his sight and followed Jesus on the way to Jerusalem. After I told this story, one little boy raised his hand. He had a very cynical look on his face, and he said, "Did that really happen?"

"Did that really happen?" I still remember that look on his face. I often see it on adults, too. It is that look which says, "Did that really happen?" "How is all of that possible?" "What kind of sign can you give me to prove all of this is true?"

"Destroy this temple and I will raise it again in three days." That is the only sign that is given to us. The resurrection of Christ confirms his Word is true. He has the power and authority to cleanse the temple and to cleanse our hearts. His power is made manifest in healing and helping, in saving and rescuing lost sinners.

As Bartimaeus discovered, Jesus can open eyes that are blind. He can also open hearts that are blind to God's goodness and grace. However, the thing to note is that Bartimaeus believed that Christ had the power to heal him. He had faith. He believed the Scriptures. He knew that this Jesus of Nazareth is the true Messiah. He is the Son of David, the divine Savior God had promised to send to his people. "Jesus, Son of David, have mercy on me!"

This becomes our prayer today also. We turn to the Son of David for healing and help, for salvation and rescue. We cry out, "Jesus, help me in my hour of need! Lord, I believe; help my unbelief. Lord Jesus, cleanse my temple and restore unto me the joy of salvation!"

Notice how John tells us the disciples did not understand what Jesus was doing that day when he cleansed the temple in Jerusalem. They did not comprehend this action by Christ and could not figure out what it all meant. Only after the resurrection did they understand.

John says, "After he was raised from the dead, his disciples recalled what he said. Then they believed the Scriptures and the words Jesus had spoken." After the resurrection, it all clicked together. Then, they understood the words Jesus had spoken on that fateful day. "Destroy this temple and I will raise it again in three days." "His disciples recalled what he said."

Some of the people present that momentous day in the temple would also remember these words. These words of Jesus would come back around again, a couple of years later, during his trial before the religious authorities. At the trial of Jesus, evidence was sought so that they could make a formal charge against him. They needed some reason to condemn Jesus to death. Ironically, the religious leaders would bring about the very sign they were seeking.

During the trial, they could not find any evidence of a crime he had committed. Finally, some people stepped forward and said, "This fellow said that he would destroy the temple of God and rebuild it in three days. He said, 'I'm going to destroy the temple!'" Then the high priest stood up and said to Jesus, "Are you not going to answer? What is this testimony that these men are bringing against you?" But Jesus remained silent.

The high priest then said to him, "I charge you under oath by the living God: Tell us if you are the Christ, the Son of God." "Yes, it is as you say," Jesus replied. "But I say to all of you: In the future, you will see the Son of Man sitting at the right hand of the Mighty One and coming on the clouds of heaven."

Then the high priest tore his clothes and said, "He has spoken blasphemy! Why do we need any more witnesses? Look, now you have heard the blasphemy. What do you think?" "He is worthy of death!" they answered. And so, Jesus is taken away to the cross. He is condemned to be executed. They crucify him because of the words he spoke.

Furthermore, as our Lord hangs upon the cross, we hear this: "The people who passed by hurled insults at him, shaking their heads and saying, 'You who were going to destroy the temple and build it in three days, save yourself! Come down from the cross, if you are the Son of God!'"

We then hear, "In the same way the chief priests, the teachers of the law and the elders mocked him. 'He saved others,' they said. 'But he can't save himself! He's the King of Israel!

Let him come down now from the cross, and we will believe in him.'"

However, the Son of God did not save himself. He did not come down from the cross. The King of Israel wears a crown of thorns as he dies for our sins. The temple of God was destroyed. The Son of David, had mercy upon us, as he poured out his life-blood to make atonement for our guilt.

The temple was destroyed, his body was put to death, his blood was shed. Then, the lifeless body of Christ was buried in the tomb; it was placed in the heart of the earth for three days. Like the great fish that swallowed the prophet Jonah, death swallowed up Jesus.

However, it turns out that death itself was then swallowed up by the resurrection of the Christ. The temple of God was rebuilt in three days. The Son of Man rose from the dead. The sign he gave was confirmed. It was all true and it all come to pass exactly as Jesus said it would.

"After he was raised from the dead, his disciples recalled what he said. Then they believed the Scriptures and the words Jesus had spoken." The same is true for us today. We also now have our sign and we have no more reason to doubt. All of this really happened, and it happened for our salvation. The temple of God is now the body of Christ, and the body of Christ is his church. We are God's temple and the Holy Spirit dwells in us. You are God's temple! And if your body is destroyed by death, our Lord will rebuild it in the resurrection on the last day. Amazing!

But wait, there is even more good news today. Today, we are privileged to eat at the King's Table. As we receive Holy Communion, we believe the Scriptures and the words that Jesus speaks: "This is my body given for you. This is my blood shed for you for the forgiveness of sins." We believe the Scriptures and receive the true body and blood of Christ.

The Holy Spirit now creates saving faith and true understanding in our hearts. It all clicks together when we comprehend that the tomb is empty. Christ has risen! Our eyes are opened, and like Bartimaeus, we now follow Jesus to Jerusalem.

Our eyes are now opened to behold our risen Savior who says, "Go! Your faith has healed you." We believe the Scriptures and rejoice in God's gifts. We put away our questions and doubts, and rest easy in God's grace. The Spirit of God dwells in our temple, and the blood of Christ cleanses us continually. Thanks be to God for his wondrous gifts! Amen!

Here is a bonus sermon from the book,
"Living in Wonder & Praise"

SOMETHING TO CELEBRATE: Zephaniah 3:14-20

Did you hear about the monastery that had a very strict rule of silence? This order of monks lived by a strict rule that permitted speaking in public only once a year, by only one monk.

When the day came around, the monk whose turn it was, stood up and said to everyone in the dining hall, "I don't like the mashed potatoes here. They are too lumpy!" And he sat down. A year later, another monk whose turn it was, stood up and said, "I rather like the mashed potatoes here. I think they are very tasty!" And he sat down. Another year went by, and it was a third monk's turn to speak. He stood up and said, "I'm leaving the monastery. I can't stand all this constant bickering!"

Today, we celebrate! We rejoice, laugh and sing. We give thanks for the birth of our Lord. Today, we have something to celebrate: The Lord is with us! Immanuel has come; the King of Israel is here. The Son of God has been born of the Virgin Mary. Thanks be to God! We have joy in Christ.

Zephaniah says, "Sing, O Daughter of Zion. Shout aloud, O Israel! Be glad with all of your heart. The Lord your God is with you, he is mighty to save. He will take great delight in you, he will quiet you with his love, he will rejoice over you with singing."

Paul says, "Rejoice in the Lord always. I will say it again: Rejoice! The Lord is near."

Matthew says, "The angel said to Joseph, 'Joseph, son of David, do not be afraid to take Mary home as your wife, because what is conceived in her is from the Holy Spirit. She will give birth to a son, and you are to give him the name Jesus, because he will save his people from their sins. And they shall call him, Immanuel, which means, God with us.'"

Our reading today tells us about our Savior. He is the King of Israel. He is Immanuel, God with us in the flesh. He is the Lord, our God, mighty to save. He is Jesus. He is conceived by the power of the Holy Spirit and born of the Virgin Mary. He comes to save us from our sins. He is mighty to save.

Zephaniah says, "The Lord has taken away your punishment. The Lord, the King of Israel is with you; never again will you fear any harm. Do not fear, O Zion, the Lord your God is with you, he is mighty to save." Zephaniah was a prophet who lived in Jerusalem around 600 BC. He lived in very difficult times. Judah had just barely survived the long, harsh reign of Manasseh.

Manasseh was an evil character and a rotten king. He totally rejected the worship of the one true God. He was a big-time idolater who dabbled in the occult and witchcraft. He persecuted and killed the true prophets of God. Manasseh loved to worship all the foreign gods of the surrounding nations, and he introduced all kinds of bizarre worship practices into Judah and Jerusalem. He filled the land with idol worship and false teachings.

Much later on, the grandson of Manasseh would be just the opposite. King Josiah was a true believer. He tried to reform the spiritual life of Judah and Jerusalem. But Josiah had his work cut out for him. He faced an incredible challenge because when people stop believing in the one true God, and when society starts falling apart, it's hard to fix things.

Manasseh had totally corrupted the moral fiber of society. He had totally decimated the worship life of Israel. The temple and the priesthood were in total disarray. Manasseh had rejected the Word of God and tried to kill all the prophets.

Manasseh was king for 55 years. But now, he is gone. Amon, his son, followed in the evil way of his father, but he only reigned two years. A new day began with the reign of Josiah, who would rule for 33 years.

The prophet Zephaniah was active during the reign of Josiah, and he seeks to encourage the new king to remain faithful to God's Word. Zephaniah wants to help revive the spiritual life of God's people. His book is a message of hope for the future. The prophet calls the people to repentance and faith.

This is why Zephaniah says, "Be glad and rejoice with all your heart, O Daughter of Jerusalem. The Lord has taken away your punishment, he has turned back your enemy. Do not fear, O Zion. The Lord your God is with you, he will quiet you with his love, he will rejoice over you with singing."

Zephaniah says, "Look, things have been bad for a long time. But we have something to celebrate! Our God is with us. He is mighty to save. No matter what may happen to us, we are always safe in his love. No matter how bad things get, there is hope for the future. There is the Living God!" Here, Zephaniah directs us to the Living God of salvation. That is our only hope in times of trouble. Our God is mighty to save. He reaches out to us in mercy and grace. God the Father sends his Son to be born of the Virgin Mary. God sends his Son to be our Savior. That is what we celebrate this Christmas.

Christmas is about Christ, the Son of God, the One who is born of Mary. He is the King of Israel who becomes flesh and blood for us. He lives our life and dies our death. Our Lord is the Messiah. He becomes true flesh and blood as he enters our world and enters our life. God himself comes to rescue his people. "The Lord your God is with you, he is mighty to save."

Matthew tells us that this birth of Jesus "took place to fulfill what the Lord had said through the prophet." You see, all the prophets of the Old Testament had predicted and promised that God would come to us. In Christ, we see the fulfillment of all of God's promises. Jesus is the one who brings hope and salvation to a dying world.

Jesus is true God and true man, all in one person. Because he is true man, he is able to take our place and live our life. He keeps the law of God on our behalf. As true man, he is able to die that death we deserve. He sheds his human blood on the cross. And because this crucified man is true God, his suffering and death have infinite value and worth. His shed blood takes away the sins of the world. God himself pays the price we owe. God himself suffers that punishment we deserve. The blood of God is shed on the cross.

As Zephaniah says, "The Lord has taken away your punishment. Be glad and rejoice with all your heart." Because of Christ, your sins are forgiven. You now have something to celebrate! God loves you, forgives you and restores to you the joy of salvation. "Rejoice in the Lord, always! I will say it again, rejoice!"

The Father sends his Son to bring you hope and comfort, peace and strength. Christ is your Savior: He is Immanuel, God with you in the flesh. And, in the words of Zephaniah, God will take great delight in you, he will quiet you with his love, he will rejoice over you with singing.

Isn't that amazing? God rejoices over you with singing. Now, as far as I know, this is the only verse in the Bible that describes God as singing. The picture here is that God loves you so much that he sings for joy. God is so glad that you belong to him, he rejoices over you and takes great delight in you.

What a wonderful message of good news! You are God's beloved child! He accepts you and loves you. He promises to be with you and to quiet you with his love. The Lord is mighty to save. He is going to help you and watch over you and bless you. He "sings over you."

Again, that is what we celebrate today. The Lord is mighty to save. The true King of Israel is with us, and he deeply loves us. He is filled with compassion and mercy. He comes to us in grace. He is Immanuel, the Christ-child cradled in the arms of Mary.

Therefore, "Be glad and rejoice with all your heart." Laugh, rejoice and sing. Be glad and filled with joy. And go and tell everyone that

God has sent us salvation. God has sent to us his Son. "Go and tell it on the mountain, that Jesus Christ is born." Go and tell everyone you know, we have something to celebrate! Amen!

Here is a bonus sermon from the book, "Christ is Our Hope"

WHAT HAPPENED THAT FRIDAY: Luke 23:26-49

I am the Roman centurion who was at the crucifixion of Jesus of Nazareth. Today, I want to tell you what happened to me on that Friday. It was a day that I will never forget.

I was in charge of three crucifixions that day. We got up there at Golgotha at 9:00 in the morning. It was pretty much business as usual. We had three criminals to execute. After all these years of doing this, I don't even blink anymore when the spikes are pounded in. You get used to it.

The day started out just like all the others. However, by the end of the day, something very profound had happened to me. After witnessing all of these incredible events that transpired on that Friday, something changed inside of me. I am a different person now.

It all began with our final victim. We had just nailed two notorious criminals to their crosses and had lifted them up, when we turned to our third guy. They called him "Jesus of Nazareth," and there was quite a group of people who had followed him up to this rocky hillside. Some of the people were weeping and some were shouting out insults. It was quite a scene. We have to push the surging crowd back before we got down to business. That is when the first remarkable thing happened.

We laid this Jesus guy down on the cross, and we tied his arms and legs to the beams. Then, as I was driving in the big spikes into his hands, he cried out in a loud voice, "Father, forgive them, for they know not what they are doing. Father, forgive them!" I was shocked. Normally, when we crucify someone, we hear cursing and profanity and swearing. We hear the criminals screaming, "I'm innocent! Let me go! I didn't do it!" But this man cried out, "Father, forgive them!" Can you believe that? He was actually asking God to forgive us as we are nailing him to the wood. Why would he say that? What kind of person is this?

We usually give our victims some wine mixed with myrrh to dull the pain a little. But this Jesus would have none of that. He didn't avoid the pain and suffering. He didn't complain, curse or resist. He accepted the cross in a way I have never seen before. And so, we crucified him. We nailed him to his cross and we hoisted it up and set it into the posthole in the ground. One of my guys got up on a ladder and nailed a placard above his head. That was unusual for us to do, but Pilate had insisted on it. This placard read: "This is the King of the Jews." We stepped back and wondered what that meant. If this guy was some kind of king, he sure didn't look like it. Then, I noticed the crown of thorns on his head. For some reason, I hadn't noticed that before. That was strange. I began to wonder, "What on earth is going on here?"

My soldiers then took the garments we had stripped off him and we divided them up by casting lots. That was our usual procedure. To the victor go the spoils, right? That's when the crowd began to get ugly. They were yelling and screaming even more. I took a close look at the crowd surrounding us, and I was shocked to see some high priests in that mob. In fact, there was quite a group of the highest religious officials of Jerusalem who had come up to this rocky hill.

You never see that. The religious authorities never come out to witness a Roman execution. It is usually just the family members of the victims, and maybe some Jewish protesters. That caught my attention. These religious leaders of Israel really had a field day. They seemed to enjoy themselves as they taunted Jesus. They yelled out, "Look at him! He saved others, but he cannot save himself! If you are the Christ, save yourself! If you are the King of Israel, come down from the cross. Then, we will believe in you!"

They said, "If you are the Son of God, save yourself! If you are the King, come down from the cross and prove it! Come on down! Save yourself! Prove you are the Messiah!" On and on it went. Even one of my guys got caught up in this. He went up to Jesus and yelled out, "If you are the king of Jews, save yourself!" The other soldiers laughed at this, but I didn't find it funny. I told them to knock it off and get back to work. All of these strange things that were being said about this man, just kind of shook me up inside. Who was this?

Did he really save others? Was he really the King of Israel? Was he the Messiah? And what's this business about him being the Son of God? What did that mean? Why would they say that?

I had heard some vague rumors that the Jews believed that God would one day send someone very special to save them. This Messiah would be a King. He would be a Savior. He might even be God himself. To be honest, I always thought that would actually be a good thing to experience. I mean, wouldn't that be great? Imagine, God sending someone to rescue us from this rotten world of pain, heartache and death. Or maybe even God himself stepping into the picture to help us out. But could that ever happen? What that even possible?

Finally, those religious big shots ran out of gas and stopped their taunting. However, the other criminals, who were crucified that day, didn't stop their endless screaming. One of them yelled at Jesus, "Aren't you the Christ? Save yourself and save us!" He kept this up for quite a while. The other criminal finally shut him down. He yelled out, "Why don't you leave him alone? Don't you fear God? We are being punished justly. We are getting what we deserve. We are guilty. But this man has done nothing wrong. He is innocent!"

I was listening to all of this, amazed. What were these guys saying? Was Jesus the Christ? Was he truly innocent? Why did he submit to this crucifixion so willingly, if he had done nothing wrong? And what did God have to do with this whole business? "Don't you fear God?" Then, things got even stranger. The one criminal who had defended Jesus, cried out to him, "Jesus, remember me when you come into your kingdom!" Then, Jesus answered him in a loud and clear voice, which everyone could hear, "I tell you the truth, today you will be with me in paradise." That statement struck me to the core. Jesus did acknowledge that he was a King, and he even welcomed this criminal into his kingdom. He promised paradise to the one who called upon him for rescue. Instead of saving himself, the crucified Christ offers salvation to a poor, lost sinner. That prayer kept ringing in my ears: "Jesus, remember me when you come into your kingdom."

It was now noon and we took a break to eat lunch. When we sat down to eat, the sky began to turn dark. We looked up at the sky and noticed there was no eclipse occurring. There were no thunderstorms nearby. In fact, it was completely still. No wind at all. That was kind of spooky. The crowds became silent now as the sky just turned black. It was eerie. Not at all like a dark night with no moon, but just some kind of supernatural darkness covering the whole land. We could still see to some degree, but it was as if the sun was completely extinguished. I felt a real sense of dread, a foreboding of what was about to happen next.

Three hours of this darkness went slowly by. We just couldn't take our eyes away from Jesus as he hung on the cross, bleeding and dying. Then, around 3:00 in the afternoon, he cried out in anguish, "My God, my God, why have you forsaken me?" That loud cry echoed through the rocky hills. I had never witnessed anything as powerful as this. The darkness now started to lighten a bit. The wind started to stir. Something was happening. I could sense it. We all held our breath. No one was moving, not even the crowds who were still hanging around.

Then Jesus lifted up his head and he shouted out, "It is finished! Father, into your hands I commit my spirit." Then, he stopped breathing. He died. We were all stunned. No one said a word. We could all see he was truly dead. I stood there, trying to figure out these last words. Something was finished. Something had been completed by this terrible death. But what? Jesus had spoken of forgiveness and paradise. Is that what he meant? It definitely sounded like he was saying, "Father, my mission is complete. My work is done! I'm coming home. I commit to you, my spirit." But what did it all mean?

At that moment, a big earthquake shook the whole area. It was mayhem up there on Golgotha as the ground shook and the rocks rolled around. Later, I heard that the big curtain inside the temple had been torn in two, from top to bottom. It was as if the hand of God had done this. I knew that curtain was quite thick. It was multiple layers of cloth. But it had been neatly torn down the middle. Incredible!

After the earthquake subsided, the sun was back to full strength. I stood there in the bright sunlight, and it was as if a light was dawning in my heart. I now realized and understood that God had sent someone special to save his people. And I immediately sensed that this salvation included all people, all who would confess that Jesus was the Lord and King. After all, that criminal prayed to Jesus for salvation, and Jesus said, "I tell you the truth, today you will be with me in paradise." If Jesus could save a guilty criminal, he could save me as well!

As I stood there, looking up at the crucified Christ, I prayed quietly under my breath, "Jesus, remember me when you come into your kingdom." I prayed that several times and then I felt the sudden urge to praise God for what had just happened. I cried out with a loud voice everyone could hear, "Surely this was a righteous man! Surely this was the Son of God!" The other soldiers standing there looked at me in astonishment. But I noticed a couple of the guys were almost nodding in agreement. I was not alone in thinking that something tremendous had just occurred. There was something very different about this man from Nazareth. He most definitely was a King, but a King like no other.

I have to admit that it took me some time to figure things out. But what I witnessed that day changed my life forever. I later learned that this Jesus of Nazareth came back to life after he was buried and sealed up in a tomb. He became alive again and he appeared to his followers. In the months after that fateful Friday, I came to know many of his followers. They told me more about this remarkable man. They filled me in about his teaching and his miracles.

Jesus of Nazareth was that promised Messiah the people of Israel were looking for. He is the one sent by the Father to save us. He is that special Savior who rescues a lost and broken world. Jesus is the true King who establishes God's kingdom. This would be a spiritual kingdom based upon God's promises and the Messiah's saving work. It would be a gift.

In this kingdom, sinners would be forgiven. In fact, that is why Jesus died on the cross. He was giving himself to pay the price for our sins. Even though he was innocent and had done nothing wrong, he was willing to become guilty and to carry our sins. He took our place and became our substitute. He was like a sacrificial lamb. He gave himself for us. That is what was happening during those three hours of that terrible darkness. Jesus was willing to suffer that punishment we deserve. He was punished by the Father, so that we might be forgiven. He was forsaken, so that we might be accepted into the kingdom. He died, so that we might live.

And there was even more good news! This man was also the Son of God. That is why his death was so powerful and effective. God himself was reconciling the whole world unto himself through Jesus. This Jesus of Nazareth was really God in the flesh. Incredible! Now I understood why he had such a profound impact upon me and everyone else that paid attention to the events of that dark Friday. "Father, forgive them!" "Today, you will be with me in paradise." "It is finished!" "Father, into your hands I commit my spirit."

I could go on, but I will end my story here. I just wanted to share with you what happened to me on that Friday, so that you might hear what I heard, and see what I witnessed with my own eyes. It changed my life, and I pray that it will change your life as well. Always remember, this is the true King, who wore that crown of thorns for our salvation. He is the King of Israel who did not come down from the cross. He gave himself for us. The Messiah completes and fulfills all of God's promises and prophecies. "It is finished!" The way to God's kingdom is now wide open. The curtain has been torn in two. We all have free access to the Almighty God, the Maker of heaven and earth. We are reconciled to our Creator. The gates to paradise are reopened.

Come now and join me in his kingdom of grace! Experience his forgiveness. If Jesus can forgive this old Roman centurion, he can also forgive you. If he can accept me, then he will accept you. Together, we can learn to pray, "Jesus, remember me when you come into your kingdom." Amen!

THEOLOGICAL TERMS

Everyone should know these definitions. Knowing the meaning of these terms, will help you understand theology better.

Absolution: The forgiveness of sins.

Angels: Creatures who were made by God to be his servants. They are not human and they are not divine. We do not pray to angels or worship them. Angels are intelligent, spiritual beings. Some of the angels rebelled against God and fell away. These are the devil and his demons.

Anoint: To set apart for a special task by applying oil. In the Old Testament, prophets, priests and kings were anointed by olive oil. Jesus was anointed by the Holy Spirit at his baptism.

Apostle: One sent forth personally by Christ to preach the gospel.

Ascension (of Christ): Forty days after Jesus rose from the dead, he ascended into heaven to prepare a place for us. He now rules with the Father. (See Right Hand of God.)

Atonement: Paying the price. By his death on the cross, Jesus atoned or paid the price for our sins. (See Propitiation, Reconciliation.)

Attribute: Anything that can be said about a person or thing. (The attributes of God are that he is eternal, all-knowing, all-powerful, all-present, etc.)

Baptism: To apply water in the name of the Father, Son and Holy Spirit for the forgiveness of sins, according to God's own promises and command.

Catholic: Literally, "universal, world-wide." The church is the holy, catholic (universal) church because it exists throughout the world.

Christ: Greek for "Anointed One." Jesus was anointed by the Holy Spirit to be our Prophet, Priest and King. (See Messiah, Anoint).

Church: All those who trust and believe in Jesus Christ as Lord and Savior.

Communion of Saints: All those who are united and joined to Christ through faith. Also known as, the Body of Christ or the Church.

Confession: (1) Admitting our sin and guilt before God; (2) A statement of belief and teachings (a confession of faith).

Congregation: A local gathering of Christians who come together for worship, Bible Study and fellowship.

Conscience: Our inner sense of right and wrong. Since the fall of Adam and Eve, the human conscience is unreliable, unless guided by the Word of God.

Contrition: Deep, heart-felt sorrow for sin.

Conversion: To be turned by God from unbelief to faith in Christ.

Covenant: An agreement God makes with us, where he promises to be our God and to bless us (also called a Testament).

Creed: A statement of belief and teaching (a confession of faith).

Death: Physical death is the separation of the soul from the body. Spiritual death is the separation from God in this life. Eternal death is the never-ending separation from God in hell. (See Heaven, Hell.)

Deity: The state of being God (Divinity).

Divine: Of, like, or from God.

Doctrine: A teaching of the Bible.

Doxology: A song of praise to God.

Election: God choosing us to be saved. Even as we now believe in Christ as our Savior, we also know that we have been chosen to eternal life, purely out of grace in Christ, without any merit of our own, and that no one can pluck us out of our heavenly Father's hand. (Known as Predestination.)

Eternal: Without beginning or end. God is eternal.

Exaltation (of Christ): To exalt is to raise high. Christ's exaltation is that as true man, he now fully and always uses his divine power and glory. (See Humiliation of Christ.)

Excommunication: The excluding from a congregation of one who will not repent of a known sin, even though they have been urged by others to do so.

Faith: (1) Putting our confidence and trust in Jesus as our only Savior. (2) A set of beliefs; what the church teaches and confesses (as in, the Christian faith).

Fall: The fall occurred when Adam and Eve disobeyed God and fell from the perfect state in which God had originally created them. The fall into sin ruined God's whole creation. Our sinful human nature is a product of the fall. (See Image of God, Original Sin.)

Flesh: The sinful human nature we were born with.

Forgiveness: To let someone go free of the guilt and punishment they deserve; not to hold against someone the wrong they have done. Christ won God's forgiveness for all people. Everyone who believes in Christ has the forgiveness of all sins.

Fulfill: To convert into actuality; to effect; to carry out; to complete; to satisfy all requirements. Jesus fulfills all of the prophecies and promises of the Bible.

Gospel: (1) The good news that God loves us and has unconditionally forgiven all of our sins. (2) The first four books of the New Testament are called the Gospels because they recount the story of Jesus, his life, death and resurrection.

Grace: The undeserved love of God for lost sinners.

Heaven: Where God is. To be in heaven means to be directly with God forever. (The final state of heaven will be a renewed creation. The entire universe shall be renewed and set free from sin and death. The Bible calls this: the New Creation, the New Heavens and Earth, or Paradise restored.)

Hell: The opposite of heaven; the state of never-ending separation from God. To be in hell means to be separated from the presence of God forever.

Holy: Without sin; something set apart for God.

Holy Communion: The true body and blood of our Lord Jesus Christ under the bread and wine, instituted by Christ himself for us to eat and drink (also known as The Lord's Supper, the Eucharist, Communion, or the Sacrament of the Altar).

Humiliation (of Christ): To humble is to bring low. Christ's humiliation was that as true God, he did not always use his divine power during his earthly ministry. (See Exaltation of Christ).

Idolatry: Having or worshipping a false god.

Image of God: The original condition of Adam and Eve when God created them. They knew and loved God directly and fully. They were righteous, holy and without sin. The Image of God was lost in the fall, but it is being restored in Christians through the work of the Holy Spirit (but it will only be fully restored in heaven).

Immortal: Undying; not subject to death.

Immutable: The state of being not subject to change. God is unchangeable.

Impenitent: Not being sorry for sin.

Impute: To charge (with sin or guilt), or to credit (with righteousness).

Incarnation: To become flesh; the taking on of a human body and soul by the Son of God, so that he is now both God and man, in one undivided person.

Iniquity: That which does not measure up to God's Law. (See Sin.)

Intercede: To pray or act for someone else. (See Mediator.)

Justification: To declare not guilty. Because of our Lord's death on the cross in place of all people, God declares all people, not guilty.

Law: The Law teaches us what God wants us to be, and to do and not to do. Because of our sinful nature, we cannot obey God's Law and keep it, and thus the Law accuses and condemns us. The Law is summed up in the Ten Commandments. (See Will of God.)

Liturgy: An order of worship.

Means of Grace: The instruments or means through which God gives out his grace and forgiveness. This includes the Word of God, Baptism and Holy Communion.

Mediator: To mediate is to intervene and help settle differences. Christ is our Mediator before God.

Messiah: Hebrew for the "Anointed One," the Christ.

Mortal: Subject to death.

Name of God: God, as he has revealed himself to us. All of the names of God in the Bible summarize everything God is, and everything he does for us. (Our God is the Creator, Maker, Savior, Lord, the Almighty, King, Redeemer, Rock, Fortress, etc.).

Natural Man: Sinful man, as he is by birth, before conversion (also called human nature, the flesh, the old Adam, the old man). (Note: Even after our conversion, we still have our sinful nature to contend with. A Christian is both a saint and sinner, at the same time.)

Obedience (of Christ): (1) the Active Obedience of Christ is that he took our place under the Law and he kept and fulfilled it for us. (2) The Passive Obedience of Christ is that he suffered and died on the cross for our guilt because we failed to keep the Law.

Omnipresent: Present everywhere. God is all-present.

Omnipotent: All-powerful and almighty. God is all-powerful.

Omniscient: All-knowing. God knows all things.

Original Sin: The sin and guilt passed on from sinful parents to their children (also called Inherited Sin). Since the fall, all human beings are born with Original Sin. All of us need God's grace and forgiveness. "Flesh gives birth to flesh."

Passion (of Christ): The physical pain and spiritual suffering Jesus experienced for our salvation.

Petition (of Prayer): Asking God for something.

Prophesy: To speak forth the Word of God; to preach; to proclaim law and gospel.

Propitiation: To make favorable; to pay the price for sins, to remove God's wrath against sin. Christ did this through his atoning death on the cross as our substitute. (See Atonement.)

Providence (of God): God's preservation, care and governing of the universe by his power, for his own wise purposes, and for the good of his creatures.

Real Presence: In Holy Communion, the true body and blood of Christ are present in, with, and under the bread and wine.

Reconciliation: To bring back together again; the removal of the barrier between God and human beings caused by our fall into sin.

Redemption: To redeem means to buy back. Redemption is the freeing of mankind from sin, death and the power of the devil through the blood of Jesus, our Redeemer.

Regeneration: To be re-born by God into a new spiritual life; to pass from spiritual death to spiritual life. (Also called the New Birth, being Born Again.)

Remit: To forgive sins.

Remission (of sins): The forgiveness of sins.

Repentance: The change of heart brought about by the Holy Spirit through God's Word. It includes both turning away from sin, and turning to God in faith.

Righteousness: To be right, just and innocent before God. The righteousness of God comes not by our performance or achievements, but only through faith in Jesus Christ. Because Jesus took our place and was our substitute, God imputes and credits righteousness to all who trust in his Son.

Right Hand of God: The exalted and ascended Christ rules over all things for the good of his church.

Sacred: Holy and set apart for God. (See Holy.)

Sacrament: A sacred act instituted by God, in which God himself has joined his Word of promise to a visible element (water, bread, wine), and by which he offers, gives, and seals the forgiveness of sins earned by Jesus

Christ. There are two sacraments: Baptism and Holy Communion.

Salutary: Giving health and salvation.

Sanctification: To make holy. The Holy Spirit sanctifies us by making our lives holy through the blood of Jesus. Our growing in holiness is an ever-ongoing process; we will reach perfection and absolute holiness only in heaven.

Sin: Anything that separates us from God; the breaking of God's Law; to rebel against and disobey God's will. (Also called Iniquity, Trespass, Transgression, Lawlessness, Debt, Disobedience, Evil, Vice, Wickedness, Wrong, Rebellion.)

Steward: A manager who takes care of something entrusted to him. We are God's stewards, and we seek to faithfully manage what he has entrusted to us.

Temptation: To be put to the test.

Theology: The study of God and his Word.

Trinity: Literally, "three-in-one." The God of the Bible is the Father and the Son and the Holy Spirit. God is three distinct persons in one divine being. Each person is true God;

yet, there are not three Gods, but one God. (Also called The Triune God, the Holy Trinity.)

Vicarious: One person acting for another. Christ, as our substitute, died for us on the cross in our place (this is called the Vicarious Atonement).

Will of God: What God wants us to do, and not to do. How God wants us to live, think and treat others. (Also: God's desire to save us: his good and gracious will.)

Word of God: God's revealing of himself in the Holy Scriptures, and in his Son, Jesus Christ (who is the Word made flesh).

Worship: God comes to us in his grace through Word and Sacrament, and we respond with our praise, prayer and thanksgiving. (Also called the Divine Service because God serves us through worship. He serves us and then we joyfully go forth to serve others.)

ABOUT THE AUTHOR:

Volker Heide has served as a pastor in the Lutheran Church – Missouri Synod for 30 years. He attended Concordia Seminary in St. Louis, Missouri (M. Div., New Testament Theology), and also the United States Merchant Marine Academy in Kings Point, New York (B.S., Nautical Science). This is his first book.

Made in the USA
Coppell, TX
06 March 2023